Angela Shelf Medearis offers interesting food and food for thought about entertaining in the Afrocentric mode."
—Jessica B. Harris, author of *The Welcome Table* and *A Kwanzaa Keepsake*

LET'S CELEBRATE

MARTIN LUTHER KING DAY
with Creole Pork Chops, Cornmeal Muffins, and Old-Fashioned Banana Pudding

AFRICAN-AMERICAN HISTORY MONTH
with Brazilian Corn and Shrimp Casserole, Caribbean New Potatoes, and Hot Southern Cider

NATIONAL MALCOLM X DAY
with Congo Chicken Moambe, Rice Dahomey Style, and Ethiopian Lentil Soup

JUNETEENTH
with Spicy West Indian Fish, Honey-Grilled Vegetables, and No-Bake Brownies

FOURTH OF JULY
with Bourbon-Glazed Baby Back Ribs, Reunion Coleslaw, and Lone-Star Potato Salad

KWANZAA
with West African Couscous, Baked Cheddar Tomatoes, Soul Food Dip, and Lemon Pecan Cake

ANGELA SHELF MEDEARIS is the author of *A Kwanzaa Celebration* (available from Dutton) and *The African-American Kitchen: Cooking from Our Heritage* (available from Plume). She lives in Austin, Texas.

Ideas for Entertaining from the African-American Kitchen

ANGELA SHELF MEDEARIS

A PLUME BOOK

PLUME
Published by the Penguin Group
Penguin Putnam Inc., 375 Hudson Street, New York, New York 10014, U.S.A.
Penguin Books Ltd, 27 Wrights Lane, London W8 5TZ, England
Penguin Books Australia Ltd, Ringwood, Victoria, Australia
Penguin Books Canada Ltd, 10 Alcorn Avenue, Toronto, Ontario, Canada M4V 3B2
Penguin Books (N.Z.) Ltd, 182–190 Wairau Road, Auckland 10, New Zealand

Penguin Books Ltd, Registered Offices: Harmondsworth, Middlesex, England

Published by Plume, an imprint of Dutton NAL,
a member of Penguin Putnam Inc.
Previously published in a Dutton edition.

First Plume Printing, October, 1998
10 9 8 7 6 5 4 3 2

Ⓟ REGISTERED TRADEMARK—MARCA REGISTRADA

The Library of Congress has catalogued the Dutton edition as follows:
Medearis, Angela Shelf.
Ideas for entertaining from the African-American kitchen / Angela Shelf Medearis.
p.   cm.
ISBN 0-525-94071-5 (hc.)
ISBN 0-452-27537-7 (pbk.)
1. Afro-American cookery.   2. Holiday cookery—United States.   3. Entertaining—
United States.   4. Menus.   I. Title.
TX715.M4825   1997
641.59'296073—dc21   97–22120
                                                                CIP

Printed in the United States of America
Original hardcover design by Eve L. Kirch

BOOKS ARE AVAILABLE AT QUANTITY DISCOUNTS WHEN USED TO PROMOTE PRODUCTS OR
SERVICES. FOR INFORMATION PLEASE WRITE TO PREMIUM MARKETING DIVISION,
PENGUIN PUTNAM INC., 375 HUDSON STREET, NEW YORK, NEW YORK 10014.

To my family and friends, who make any occasion a special celebration, and especially for my husband, Michael, Patricia Robinson, and Jennifer Moore, whose help, advice, and patience have been invaluable to me while writing this book. I love ya'll.

—A.S.M.

CONTENTS

Contents

INTRODUCTION

What is not recorded is not preserved, and what is not preserved is lost forever. Through *Ideas for Entertaining from the African-American Kitchen*, I am trying to do my part to preserve, share, and enlighten others about the wonderful history behind African-American celebrations and recipes. Many of the ingredients in my recipes are direct culinary contributions that Africans made to American cooking, such as black-eyed peas (which many Africans called cowpeas); sweet potatoes (which some of our ancestors substituted for African yams); okra (which was called gumbo); peanuts (which were called goobers); and sesame seeds (which were called benne in many African regions). When you use this book to help celebrate distinct African-American holidays and to infuse other holidays with an Afro-centric flair, you are cooking up a piece of history.

Africans and African-Americans have a reputation for hospitality. Good food and entertaining are integral parts of our cultural heritage. In ancient Africa, it was unthinkable not to offer a guest something to eat or drink, and many African greetings stem from some form of the question "Have you eaten?" Visitors were never pressed about the reason for their journey until they had been fed, and if it was late, they were given a place to sleep. Nothing else was so important that it could not wait until after the comfort of a guest had been assured.

Those customs survived the Middle Passage and continued throughout slavery. Even in the midst of the worst times, we offered our company our best. Peter Smith, a runaway slave from Tennessee, stated that "he pursued his journey for several days unmolested, and without eating, until he again met with some colored friends, (slaves) who gave him some victuals, and advised him to push forward." After reaching Canada and freedom, Smith issued this invitation to his former owner:

> He would not return evil for evil. But if his Master would come to Canada and visit him, he would treat him well, and give him an hospitable entertainment of a freeman.

After Emancipation, we continued to share what little we had with each other. Historian Lerone Bennett, Jr., wrote in his book *Before the Mayflower* that "in the related sphere of social welfare, the freedman played a major role in providing relief for black indigents. Many, perhaps most, of the large number of black orphans were taken in by black families, and black churches and social organizations raised thousands of dollars for social welfare and black schools." John de Forest, a Freedmen's Bureau officer in South Carolina, observed that the freedmen "were extravagant in giving."

During the trying times of segregation, it was often impossible to find a hotel or restaurant that would serve African-Americans. Traveling from one city to another was quite an adventure. People had to rely on the hospitality of the African-American community in order to find food and lodging.

Introduction

I've often heard stories of a hostess opening her back door to find a silent offering from a neighbor of a cake or pie because company had arrived and caught the hostess unprepared. It would have been unthinkable to turn the guest away without "setting a good spread."

Today delicious food attractively prepared is an important part of many celebrations, but it has always been significant in African-American celebrations. Even in these hectic modern times, gathering together with friends and family is a vital part of our community. In my family, we use any excuse for a party. After reading this cookbook, I hope you'll be inspired to entertain a little more often. Whether you're planning a gathering after a commemorative service for Dr. Martin Luther King, Jr.; hosting a rehearsal dinner for a June wedding; in charge of the next family reunion; or need tips for preparing a menu for a Kwanzaa Karamu feast in December, this cookbook is chock-full of ideas, recipes, tips for setting the table, entertainment suggestions, and history. There are also quotes to inspire you and get you through the stressful times that inevitably arise whether you're entertaining two people or two hundred.

I hope you'll learn from my party-planning mistakes, benefit from my experience, add some new recipes to your cooking repertoire, and have as much fun as I've had entertaining friends and family over the years.

Health and Happiness,
Angela Shelf Medearis, 1997

Planning the Party

There is no excuse for not having a great party. My husband, Michael, and I had wonderful parties in our teeny-tiny two-bedroom house with ragged furniture and paper plates when we first got married, and more than two decades later we've had equally wonderful parties in our new spacious house. Through the years we've always kept the same attitude: We don't give a party to show off our fancy furniture (or lack thereof) or to impress anyone. We throw parties to have and to enjoy good food with friends. Keep that in mind, and your parties are guaranteed to be a success. Also keep in mind that everyone makes mistakes; I still do and always will, and so will you. Don't dwell on the mishaps, just the wonderful memories.

If this is your first party, keep it simple, and don't be afraid to take charge and direct folks as needed. Be calm and act like you entertain all the time. For beginners, a small dinner party or informal gathering is best. You can branch out as your confidence increases. A genuine smile and a friendly spirit is the finest dress for a party and anything you prepare with love is the finest food.

I haven't been single for more than twenty-three years, but I still

think one of the best ways to gather a large group of single men together is to throw a party around a sports event. Don't forget that old
saying about the way to a man's heart. Just serve something that is
filling, tasty, and easy to eat in front of the television. And don't forget dessert.

Another one of my favorite party themes is a good cause. One
year, a friend of ours was running for political office and our local
school libraries needed new books. My sister Marcy and I hosted
a Books and Ballots fundraiser that provided money for two good
causes, and allowed us to meet others who share our interests in lit-
eracy and politics.

Some of the gatherings outlined in *Entertaining Ideas* are small,
family gatherings. Others involve a large number of guests. All of the
menus are simple, which frees you up to spend most of your time
with your guests rather than in the kitchen.

No matter what type of party you're planning, the event should
reflect your personal style. Adding cultural touches makes the gathering even more unique, and personally enriching. Enjoy yourself
and you'll find your guests will enjoy themselves too.

Before The Guests Arrive

Determine Who, What, When, and Where

Check the local calendar of events when deciding on the date for
your party. It's best to choose a date that won't conflict with another
major event. Determine the number of guests according to your budget and the amount of space you have available. Make a guest list,
with addresses and phone numbers.

Decide on a Budget

Figure out how much it will cost to buy the invitations, food, and decorations, and if needed, to rent extra serving equipment or chairs and tables. If you are hosting the party outside of your home, add in the cost of the party place. Hiring help—whether it's a baby-sitter, a bartender, or someone to serve the food and help with cleanup—is another additional cost. Consider hiring high school or college students for these jobs because they'll be less expensive than party professionals. To find students, place an ad in a local newspaper or call the school guidance counselors.

Another way to save money is to make as many things as you can yourself, such as the food and the invitations. Remember to get quotes in advance for all outside services.

Make a List

A list helps to focus your thinking and acts as a handy reminder throughout the party-planning process. Make a list of everything you need to do and to buy, consult it often, and check off the tasks as you finish them.

Do as much as you can ahead of time. Set out a few tasks to complete every day—even little things like refilling salt and pepper shakers and sugar bowls. The more you take care of in advance, the less frazzled you will be on the day of the party and the more time you will be able to spend with your guests.

Prepare and Send the Invitations

Creative, hand-written invitations are fine for gatherings of fifty people or less. Use blank cards with African-American art on the front that fits the theme of your party. Inside write all of the important information such as the date (put the day and the date, i.e., Sunday, May 26), time, place, theme, dress code, and directions. Also indicate what type of food you plan to serve. For example, "Join us after the community Kwanzaa celebration from 8:30 PM for drinks and dessert." Or "In celebration of Martin Luther King, Jr.'s, Birthday, join us for cocktails and appetizers at 6 PM, dinner promptly at 7 PM."

Once we invited everyone we could think of for a spur-of-the-moment Kwanzaa party in celebration of the holiday, our new house, and my *Kwanzaa Celebration* cookbook. I sent out tons of invitations, which I made with the book jacket as the cover, about two weeks before the event. Although I included an RSVP, I didn't get much response and I didn't verify my guest list. I should have. Nearly everyone I invited showed up and it was elbow to elbow, with folks in almost every room of the house. We didn't run out of food and we had a great time, but from now on I'll try to get a head count in advance to save us some anxiety.

For informal gatherings with a small number of guests, a phone call rather than written information is often fine, although if nothing is in writing, the guests have nothing to refer to later to verify the time, date, and other important information. You may want to call two or three weeks in advance. This will give you an idea of who will be coming so you can determine the amount of food you need to serve and the amount of space you'll need. Then one week or so before the party, you can send out a detailed, written invitation with "Regrets

Only" and a phone number. You've already spoken to your guests once, so an RSVP should not be necessary.

For large, formal gatherings, send out printed invitations four to six weeks in advance and request an RSVP. You might want to include your phone number or, to make life simpler for all concerned, a pre-printed, stamped postcard that can be used as a reply card. (If you've had a poor response and are still unsure of the number of guests to expect a week or two before the party, consider enlisting the help of a friend to call your guests for confirmation.)

If you do not want gifts, print on the invitation a simple statement, such as "No gifts except that of your presence," or "We want your presence but not your presents."

I also like to include on the invitation as much information as possible about the party theme. Information about the type of dress, such as formal, semi-formal, or casual saves embarrassment all around. A small map or detailed directions along with the invitation is invaluable if you are inviting people from out of town. State on your invitation that the party will start about thirty minutes to one hour before you want to serve the main meal (offer drinks and appetizers beforehand). That should give even the inevitable latecomers enough time.

Uninvited Children

If you don't want children at your party, say so on the invitation. If guests show up with their children anyway, you have the right to politely request that they keep their children with them at all times. You are not obligated to entertain their children or baby-sit them. If you have children of your own and are planning to hire a baby-sitter for the evening, you may want to make arrangements with your sitter to also watch the children of your guests. It will then be your obligation to pay the sitter to watch all the children that come to the party.

Plan the Menu

I never have parties that don't involve food. I don't see the point in gathering a bunch of folks together and feeding them peanuts and chips and sending them off to search for someplace else to eat. Hungry people bring bad vibes and are cranky, and I don't want cranky folks at my party. If you invite people over, have something substantial on hand to feed them. If you're hosting a cocktail party, serve appetizers that will sustain your guests for at least a couple of hours.

If you have invited your guests for a meal, put together a good all-purpose menu or use the menus suggested in this book. Figure out the amount of food you'll need to feed your guests. Compile a grocery list and do your shopping a day or two ahead of time, rather than on the day of the party. This will give you an opportunity to prepare most of the dishes in advance. It will also give you more time to take care of last-minute details on the day of your party, including a quick trip to the store if you have forgotten anything. Always buy enough lettuce and vegetables to make a huge salad. If you have really picky eaters or dieters, they can fill in the blanks with salad during the main course.

I know the eating habits of most of the people I invite and some of my friends are vegetarians. I prepare several substantial vegetarian side dishes that they use as a main course. I must admit, though, that if I had company coming from Mars, I'd probably serve chicken. I call chicken the "global bird" because I've found recipes for preparing it in almost every culture. If you don't have any idea about the culinary habits of your guests, chicken and a few hearty vegetable dishes are good choices. Keep a couple of gallons of ice cream and different toppings and nuts on hand. If you have a dessert disaster, ice cream in an attractive dish is an easy fill-in.

Prepare the Party Room

The day before your party, clean your home from top to bottom, or hire someone to do it for you. There's no telling where your guests may wander and if every room is clean, you'll have nothing to fear. Stock up the bathroom your guests will be using with "emergency" items, including safety pins, aspirin, and sanitary products. It will save everyone embarrassment and time.

Decorate your party in keeping with the theme or time of year. Decorations will help to set the tone of the party.

Set out bowls or plates of "nibbles," such as peanuts, candies, fruit sections, olives, crackers and cheese, and fresh vegetables. If you're serving liquor, set up a self-serve "bar" in a corner of the room where your guests will be seated. A card table draped with a tablecloth is fine. Place a pitcher of ice water, a bucket of ice, glasses, napkins, and bowls of lemon and lime slices on the table along with the liquor and mixers. Include non-alcoholic beverages, such as sodas, juices, and mineral water. This will free you from serving drinks while you are trying to greet newcomers or prepare dinner.

Set the Table

We eat first with our eyes, so a pretty table setting is important. If you have two sets of china with different patterns and are expecting more than six guests, alternate the plates and tie everything together with napkins and a tablecloth in a color common to both patterns. You don't have to have expensive china or crystal to set a beautiful table. Sturdy plastic (not paper) plates, plastic forks, knives, and spoons, and a tablecloth and napkins in a matching pattern can make a beautiful setting. You can buy beautiful faux crystal/plastic plates, bowls, and serving platters fairly inexpensively at party stores. Plastic serving dishes also come in a variety of colors and in beautiful shapes. I take plastic dishes when I travel around doing cooking demonstrations and they hold up very well. For one Kwanzaa celebration, I used a combination of red, black, and green plastic platters and plates with great success.

The rules for setting a table are pretty standard. The salad fork is placed to the far left of the plate. The dinner fork is next, nearest the plate. You can place your napkin on the left or use it as a decoration by arranging it in a wineglass. You can also put the salad fork on the salad plate.

Place the knife to the right of the plate, then, moving away from the plate, the teaspoon and then the soup spoon. If you are serving seafood and using a cocktail fork, place it to the right of the last spoon.

The water glass sits to the right of the plate, next to the tip of the knife. One or two wineglasses (use two if two wines are being served) are also placed to the right, but slightly in front of the plate. Remove the first wineglass as soon as the second wine is served.

Sometimes butter plates and knives and dessert forks and spoons are placed on the table, depending on the type of dinner. The butter plate is placed to the left, at the tip of the fork. The butter knife is placed across the butter plate. (For formal dinners, the butter plate and knife are not used.) The dessert fork and spoon may be served on the plate with the dessert (American style) or they may, instead, be placed on the table above the dessert plate (European style).

Set the Mood

Play soft music to set the mood. Choose civil rights hymns for the Martin Luther King Day celebration, or Kwanzaa music with lyrics that reflect each of the principles during that holiday. Billie Holiday's greatest hits will set the tone for the Blue Monday Party, and old-fashioned spirituals can be played during the Christmas celebration. Music definitely warms up a room.

Consider using brilliantly patterned African fabric as a tablecloth, protecting the fabric, if desired, with a thin sheet of clear plastic. If the cloth isn't long enough, place a longer piece of fabric or paper tablecloth in a complementary color underneath it.

Brightly colored African baskets and pottery make great serving dishes if you place plastic liners inside of them. (Liners come in all different sizes and can be purchased at party stores.) And pretty African baskets filled with fruits and vegetables in different shapes and colors, as well as African sculptures or decorative items can work well as centerpieces; just make sure they aren't too tall or too wide for the table. If you have a nice yard, you may be able to find some pretty leaves, or blooming branches on your trees that can be trimmed and placed around the centerpieces.

Flowers always brighten a room. You may want to purchase an arrangement from a florist or simply buy individual flowers and arrange them yourself. Candles and soft lighting cast the room in an elegant light and hide a multitude of flaws. Put pink light bulbs in your lamps instead of the harsh white ones. Scented candles serve two purposes, light and scent. The candle holders don't have to match or be the same height. Variety adds interest.

Breaking the Ice

If you have guests who don't know each other, introduce them and mention something that they have in common (such as children, hobbies, or mutual friends). This will get the conversation going and allow you to attend to other guests.

If your guests offer to help, let them. There are always plenty of last-minute tasks such as putting ice into glasses and folding napkins. I don't know why everyone likes to congregate in the kitchen during a party, but they do. Put as many people to work as possible and throw the rest of them out with a promise that they can help serve the food or clean up when the party is over.

Latecomers and No-Shows

If you know guests will be late or if guests haven't called and are so late that you no longer expect them, remove their place settings from the table. If they show up later, you can always reset. You are not obligated to wait on latecomers if you told everyone in advance the definite time at which you planned to serve.

Serving the Food

My favorite ways to serve guests are family-style for small groups and buffet-style for large ones. For family-style meals, guests can either serve themselves directly from the pans and bowls in the kitchen and then take their plates to the dining area, or you can set bowls of food out on the table and have your guests pass them around. If desired, choose a few of your guests to help you with serving and ask the rest to be seated.

If you are serving buffet-style, whether ten guests or one hundred, follow the basic principles that follow. They do not change regardless of the size of your gathering.

1. Arrange Food by Type

Keep all the cold foods together, the hot foods together, and the side dishes together. Set up your serving line so that guests get to the less expensive foods first (i.e., bread, salads, and side dishes, followed by the meat). Plates fill up quickly and most people don't want to pile a mountain of food onto one plate. By setting up your serving line from inexpensive to expensive you will ensure that there will be enough of the expensive food to go around.

2. Make Your Buffet Attractive

When setting up your buffet, make sure everything looks appealing. Use serving trays of different shapes together and some serving items with legs; alternate large bowls with platters; give trays height by setting them on top of sturdy boxes hidden under the tablecloth; and use a tall coffee urn and a round punch bowl to make the buffet table look interesting visually. Also, make sure you vary the colors of the foods (you don't want to put the yellow corn and the yellow squash side by side). Only use edible garnishes such as lettuce leaves, parsley, tomatoes, mushrooms, and red and green bell peppers around or on top of the food. You'd be surprised how many folks will mistake a plastic decoration for something edible.

3. Keep the Food Coming

Even for large groups I like to put the food in medium-sized bowls and platters and to continually refill them. When I put large amounts of food in large bowls I find that people tend to take more food than they can actually eat and a lot goes to waste. I prefer to inspire people to take smaller portions, always inviting them back to the buffet table for second helpings.

4. Keep Things Flowing Smoothly

Pay attention to the traffic pattern when setting up for a large group. Make sure that there is enough room for guests to move around the table and for you to get to the serving bowls so that you can refill them. I have a long hallway leading to the kitchen and a long bar in my house. I usually line large groups up in the hallway and let them serve themselves from the bar. Then I invite them to sit down to eat in the breakfast room, family room, or living or dining room. In rooms where there is no obvious dining table I set out TV trays so that there's always a place to set down plates and drinks. I also set out an ample supply of coasters. All of this works together to keep my guests comfortable and my furniture free of stains.

If you only have one table and a large group, use card tables for the main dishes. After everyone has been served, remove the main dishes and replace with the dessert. You can place the coffee, punch, cups, glasses, and ice on another card table, a little distance away. Guests seem to get up more often to refill their glasses than to refill their plates.

If you only have a small area to party in, it's best to move out as many unneeded items as possible and, if necessary, borrow, rent, or buy folding chairs and card tables. Drape the tables with matching tablecloths and decorate them in keeping with your theme. Don't crowd the room; make sure there is plenty of space for people to move around freely.

For groups of fifty or more and events held in community halls or other large centers, set up serving tables. Bear in mind that exits should not be blocked and the traffic should flow freely back and forth from the eating areas to the serving areas.

- *Center Tables, Against Wall, or L-Shaped:* One long decorated serving table can be placed in the center of the room or close to a wall (with enough room for servers to move behind it when bringing out more food or cleaning up). You may also put two tables together to make one L-shaped table near two corner walls. All the food, drinks and desserts are placed on this table.

- *Circular:* Serving tables are set up in a circle, leaving a small opening for the servers to refill bowls and platters. Guests move around the outside of the circle to serve themselves. The plates and silverware control the traffic pattern so make sure that they are placed in an area that is easily accessible and spacious enough for a line.

- *T-Shape or U-Shape table set-up:* Tables are placed in a T or U-shape. For this type of set-up it's good to have the plates, silverware, punch, coffee, and cups on either ends of the top of the T or the U on both sides of the table. This guides the guests in the direction you want them to move. The bottom of the T or U should be closest to the area where the guests sit down to eat.

- *Satellite Tables:* This arrangement works well if you want to group foods of the same type (such as appetizers, entrees, and side dishes) on the same table, placing the tables a short distance away from each other.

- *Test the Buffet.* Before inviting your guests to begin eating, do a test run of the buffet. Make sure that everything is on the table (or tables), easily accessible, and not in a precarious position, such as too close to the edge of the table. Also make sure that every dish is equipped with a serving spoon.

Last-Minute Checks

Check the bathrooms for cleanliness. Check your appearance. I'm often so busy before a party, I don't notice that my hair needs to be re-combed or my clothes are stained. Relax in the quiet before the storm. All you can do has been done. Make a joke about imperfections and enjoy the praise for everything that works out well. Most of all, have a good time. Life's too short to worry about the small stuff.

January

Emancipation Day—Jubilee Dinner Party

On December 31, 1862, African-Americans all over the country gathered together in churches to pray out the old year and pray in a new year of freedom, the year of Jubilee. Watch Services, as these end-of-the-year church meetings came to be known, are still common occurrences on New Year's Eve, however, the services held at the close of the year in 1862 were particularly prayerful ones. Heavenly appeals for the earthly freedom of African-Americans from the tyranny of slavery were fervently whispered.

On January 1, 1863, at a rally at Boston's Tremont Temple led by statesman, abolitionist, and newspaper editor Frederick Douglass, everyone eagerly awaited a telegram bearing the news of Lincoln's Emancipation Proclamation. Hopes were failing as hour after hour passed with no news from Washington. Suddenly a man ran into the room screaming, "It's coming! It's on the wires!" Despair turned into joy as the telegram containing the Emancipation Proclamation was read. The celebration lasted all night.

If one of your New Year's resolutions was to start entertaining, this simple dinner party menu in honor of Emancipation Day is a good way to start. If your house is already decorated for Christmas, Kwanzaa, or both, take advantage of it and continue the theme when setting your dinner table. Serving family-style is an easy and informal way to make sure everyone is well fed. Eat a few of the black-eyed peas in the appetizer recipe for luck, relax, and celebrate the hard-earned freedoms African-Americans now enjoy.

EMANCIPATION DAY— JUBILEE DINNER PARTY

DRINK, APPETIZER, AND SALAD

Apricot Fruit Punch

Mushroom Caps Stuffed with Black-Eyed Peas

Cucumber and Green Onion Salad

MAIN DISH

Baked Salmon Steaks

SIDE DISH

Broccoli-Parmesan Noodles

BREAD AND DESSERT

Herb Bread

Jubilee Peach Crisp

Apricot Fruit Punch

Yield: 3 quarts

"Power concedes nothing without demand; it never has and it never will." — Frederick Douglass

    2 12-ounce cans apricot nectar, chilled
1½ quarts apple cider, chilled
1½ cups orange juice, chilled
¾ cup freshly squeezed lemon juice
½ cup sugar

Combine the apricot nectar, apple cider, orange juice, lemon juice, and sugar in a large punch bowl and mix until well blended. Serve over ice.

QUICK TIP: *Clean up after yourself as you work. If you have a small dishwasher and a large crowd, load and run the dishwasher between courses. This will keep a clean supply of dishes on hand and keep your kitchen from looking like a disaster area when dinner is over. It's also a good idea to fill a sink with hot, soapy water so that you can wash items as needed.*

Mushroom Caps Stuffed with Black-Eyed Peas

Yield: 4 Servings

This is a tasty and unusual way to serve black-eyed peas, a food our ancestors introduced to American cuisine. This easy appetizer upholds an old tradition of serving black-eyed peas for luck on New Year's Day.

16 large mushrooms
 1 cup canned black-eyed peas, drained
 6 ounces ham, finely chopped (packaged ham works fine)
 2 tablespoons finely chopped green bell pepper
 2 tablespoons finely chopped yellow onion
 4 tablespoons butter, melted
 1/4 cup grated Monterey Jack cheese

Preheat the broiler. Wipe the dirt off the mushrooms with a damp paper towel. Do not wash them as the mushrooms will absorb too much of the water. Remove the stems. Place the mushroom caps on a baking sheet.

Combine the black-eyed peas, ham, bell pepper, onion, and butter in a medium bowl. Using a teaspoon, fill the mushroom caps with the pea mixture. Sprinkle the cheese on top. Place the filled mushroom caps underneath the broiler for 3 to 5 minutes to heat. Serve warm.

Cucumber and Green Onion Salad

Yield: 4 Servings

You may want to try a salad green other than iceberg lettuce for this recipe. Radicchio, arugula, or Belgian endive mixed with Boston, Bibb, or Romaine greens provide a tasty accompaniment for the cucumber mixture.

> 1   large cucumber, thinly sliced
> 1/4   cup thinly sliced green onion (tops included)
> 2   tablespoons distilled white vinegar
> 2   tablespoons virgin olive oil
> 1/2   teaspoon salt
> 1/2   teaspoon freshly ground black pepper
> 1/4   teaspoon sugar
>   Shredded lettuce or salad greens
> 4   cherry tomatoes

Combine the sliced cucumbers, green onion, vinegar, oil, salt, pepper, and sugar in a medium bowl. Place the salad greens on the plates. Spoon the cucumber mixture on top. Place a cherry tomato on top of the cucumbers. Serve cold or at room temperature.

Baked Salmon Steaks

Yield: 4 Servings

Placing the crumb mixture on the fish prevents it from drying out during the baking process and is also tasty and attractive.

- 2 **cups soft bread crumbs**
- 4 **tablespoons butter or margarine, softened**
- ½ **cup chopped celery**
- ¼ **cup chopped yellow onion**
- ¼ **cup chopped green bell pepper**
- ¼ **teaspoon sage**
- ¼ **teaspoon salt**
- 4 **salmon steaks (fresh or frozen and thawed), ¾ inch thick**

Preheat the oven to 350 degrees. Combine the bread crumbs, butter, celery, onion, bell pepper, sage, and salt together in a medium bowl. Place the salmon steaks in a nonstick baking pan or a baking pan lightly greased with a tablespoon of butter or margarine. Spread the crumb mixture thickly on top of each steak. Bake for 30 to 35 minutes (about 10 minutes per pound) until the fish is cooked through and the crumb mixture is golden brown.

Broccoli-Parmesan Noodles

Yield: 4 to 6 Servings

In this recipe the noodles and the broccoli are cooked together, which means there is one less pot than usual to wash. For the best flavors, buy your Parmesan cheese in a wedge and grate it just before you are ready to sprinkle it over the noodle mixture.

> 3 quarts water
> 1 tablespoon salt
> 1 12-ounce package medium egg noodles
> 1 10-ounce package frozen chopped broccoli
> 1/2 cup butter or margarine, melted
> 1 clove garlic, mashed and diced
> 1 teaspoon freshly ground black pepper
> 1/4 cup chopped fresh parsley
> 1/4 cup grated Parmesan cheese

Combine the water and salt in a large pot and bring to a boil. Add the egg noodles and broccoli. Cook, uncovered, until the noodles and broccoli are tender, about 7 to 10 minutes. Drain well in a colander or sieve. Do not rinse. Pour into a serving bowl. Pour the butter over the noodle mixture. Add the garlic, pepper, and parsley, tossing gently. Sprinkle with the Parmesan cheese. Serve warm.

Herb Bread

Yield: 6 to 8 Servings

A fresh, crusty loaf of French bread works best in this recipe because it won't become soggy when spread with the butter mixture.

1 (about 24 inches long) loaf unsliced French bread
1/3 cup butter or margarine, softened
1 teaspoon Worcestershire sauce
2 teaspoons chopped fresh parsley
1/2 teaspoon dried whole basil
1 clove garlic, peeled and mashed

Preheat the oven to 350 degrees. Slice the French bread crosswise into 1-inch slices and place on a large sheet of aluminum foil. In a small bowl, combine the butter, Worcestershire sauce, parsley, basil, and garlic. Spread the mixture on one side of the bread slices. Reassemble the loaf and wrap with foil. Bake for 15 minutes, or until the loaf is heated through and the butter is melted.

Jubilee Peach Crisp

Yield: 6 to 8 Servings

Save the peach juice from this recipe and add it to your punch.

1 **29-ounce can sliced peaches, drained**
1 **cup Bisquick biscuit mix**
³/₄ **cup firmly packed brown sugar**
¹/₂ **teaspoon ground cinnamon**
2 **tablespoons butter or margarine, softened**
   Vanilla ice cream or whipped cream, for serving

Preheat the oven to 400 degrees. Arrange the peach slices in an ungreased 8-inch baking pan. Combine the biscuit mix, brown sugar, and cinnamon in a large bowl and mix well. Using a fork or pastry blender, cut the butter into the biscuit mixture until it resembles cornmeal. Sprinkle the mixture over the peaches. Bake, uncovered, for 18 to 20 minutes or until the top is golden brown. Serve warm with ice cream or whipped cream.

An Afrocentric Baby Shower

Although traditional American baby showers are fun, adding Afrocentric touches to your shower will make the event even more meaningful.

Many American baby showers are all-female gatherings. Inviting the father and other male friends and acquaintances to be a part of the celebration is more in keeping with African celebrations of childbirth. My sister Marcia hosted a coed baby shower for a friend of ours. At first the men were a little confused about why they had been invited, but the party turned out to be a lot of fun, as well as a unique bonding experience for the parents.

I've always loved the section in Alex Haley's book *Roots* in which he described the celebration of childbirth practiced in the village of Juffure, in West Africa, the place where he believed his ancestors were born. This practice is called an "outdooring" ceremony in parts of West Africa and according to ancient custom, takes place on the eighth day of the child's life. Haley describes the ceremony as follows:

When the eighth day arrived, the villagers gathered in the early morning before the hut of Omoro and Binta. On their heads, the women of both families brought calabash containers of the ceremonial sour milk and sweet munko cakes of pounded rice and honey ... The alimamo [religious leader] said a prayer over the calabashes of sour milk and munko cakes, and as he prayed, each guest touched a calabash brim with his or her right hand, as a gesture of respect for the food. Then the alimano turned to pray over the infant, entreating Allah to grant him long life, success in bringing credit and pride and many children to his family, to his village, to his tribe—and, finally the strength and the spirit to deserve and to bring honor to the name he was about to receive ... Moving to his wife's side, he [Omoro] lifted up the infant and, as all watched, whispered three times into his son's ear the name he had chosen for him. It was the first time the name had ever been spoken as this child's name, for Omoro's people felt that each human being should be the first to know who he was.

"The first child of Omoro and Binta Kinte is named Kunta!" cried Brima Cesay ...

Out under the moon and stars, alone with his son that eighth night, Omoro completed the naming ritual. Carrying little Kunta in his strong arms, he walked to the edge of the village, lifted his baby up with his face to the heavens, and said softly, "Fend kiling dorong leh warrata ka iteh tee." (Behold—the only thing greater than yourself.)

In my family, after we had our children and the last portion of their umbilical cord had detached, my mother always insisted that we bury it in the backyard. I thought it was superstitious and I didn't do it for my daughter, although my sister did for hers. Later some African friends explained that burying the umbilical cord and celebrating afterward is an old West African custom. My mother's tradition of burying that small piece of the umbilical cord started in our ancestral homeland. I'm always amazed how traditions survive.

You may want to include some of the activities described by Haley as part of your Afrocentric baby shower. Or you may want to celebrate after the umbilical cord has come off. Drums always announce special events in Africa, so you may want to play a recording of African drum music. Have the oldest male offer a special blessing for the baby at the beginning of the ceremony, then at the end have the father lift the new baby to the heavens and repeat Omoro's blessing.

And don't forget the food! My African friends tell me that after the baby loses its umbilical cord the elder women prepare a big feast.

Including dishes from Africa as a part of your Afrocentric baby shower is a wonderful cultural touch. A version of the munko cakes Haley wrote about are included as part of the menu suggested here. Sour milk is one of the ingredients in the Brown-Sugar Spice Cake. I designed this menu so that your guests will not only consume a wonderful meal, they'll also learn a little more about African and African-American history.

AFROCENTRIC BABY SHOWER MENU

DRINKS AND APPETIZERS

Fruit Punch

Sweet Potato Soup

Peanuts Piri-Piri

MAIN DISHES

Nigerian Roasted Pepper Chicken

Chickpea Curry

SIDE DISH

West African–Style Spinach with Okra

DESSERT

Nigerian-Style Munko

Frosted Brown-Sugar Spice Cake

Fruit Punch

Yield: About 5 quarts

5 cups water
2 cups sugar
2 cups strong Orange Pekoe or Lemon Zest tea
  (made with about 3 tea bags)
2 cups orange juice
2 cups white grape juice
1 cup freshly squeezed lemon juice
2 quarts ginger ale
1 pint lemon-lime sherbet, softened

Combine 2 cups of the water and the sugar in a medium saucepan. Bring the mixture to a boil, stirring constantly, until it thickens into a syrup, 5 to 8 minutes. Cool.

In a large punch bowl, stir together the syrup, tea, and orange, grape, and lemon juices until well blended. Add the remaining 3 cups water and the ginger ale. Add the sherbet to the punch just before serving.

QUICK TIP: *Preparing and serving the food buffet-style is one of the easiest ways to ensure your guests are well fed, and you aren't over-worked. See pages 17–20 for tips on setting up a buffet-style dinner.*

Sweet Potato Soup

Yield: 8 to 10 Servings

Yams are an important ingredient in African cooking. Long, white African yams are not usually carried in American grocery stores, so for this traditional African soup I substitute sweet potatoes. Some Asian markets and specialty stores carry a variety of white African yams, such as cocoyams, wateryams, or white yams.

Some Nigerians believe that eating white yams will make a woman have twins, a sign of luck! However, I've happily eaten many white yams without any change in the size of my household. This soup is easy to make a day ahead of time and actually tastes better after it has rested for a while. If making a day ahead, cover and refrigerate after you add the tomato paste, lemon juice, and sherry or water. Reserve some of the chicken broth to thin the soup during the reheating process or add a little extra sherry or water.

3   pounds sweet potatoes (about 4 medium), peeled and diced
3   14.5-ounce cans chicken broth
1   tablespoon curry powder
1   teaspoon salt
1   teaspoon freshly ground black pepper
1/4   cup tomato paste
2   tablespoons freshly squeezed lemon juice
1/4   cup dry sherry or water
      Freshly shredded cilantro (coriander) leaves (optional)

Place the potatoes and broth in a large soup pot. Bring to a boil, then cover and reduce the heat to a simmer. Cook until the potatoes are fork-tender, about 15 to 20 minutes. Use a slotted spoon to remove the potatoes from the broth and retain the broth. Place the potatoes in a food processor or blender or you can mash them in a bowl with a potato masher. Add the curry powder, salt, pepper, and 1 cup of the chicken broth and blend until smooth. Pour the puréed mixture back into the pot containing the chicken broth. Add the tomato paste, lemon juice, and sherry. Cook the soup over medium heat for about 8 minutes, stirring occasionally. If the soup is too thick, add more broth, water, or sherry. Ladle into soup bowls and sprinkle with the cilantro leaves.

Peanuts Piri-Piri

Yield: 8 Servings

Peanuts have been a part of African and African-American culinary history for hundreds of years. Africans used peanuts in everything from main dishes to desserts and continued to cook with them frequently when they arrived in America. The ingenuity of African cooks and the scientific experiments conducted by Dr. George Washington Carver, which uncovered the more than 300 commercial uses of peanuts, made them an important crop in America.

It has been hard to determine exactly where the name piri-piri, or pili-pili, as it is known in some parts of Africa, originated. Some say it is a Portuguese word for the small red malagueta pepper. Others say it is a West African name for a small red peppercorn common to that region. In Mozambique, piri-piri is the name of the sauce used to coat nuts, beans, and plantains, which are eaten by the handful as snacks. This spicy party treat can be made several days ahead of time and reheated.

> 2　tablespoons vegetable oil
> 1　clove garlic, peeled and mashed
> 1　teaspoon chili powder
> 1　pound shelled peanuts
> 2　tablespoons freshly squeezed lemon juice
> ½　teaspoon salt

Heat the oil in a frying pan over high heat. Add the garlic and chili powder, then reduce the heat to medium and cook, stirring constantly, for 2 minutes. Add the peanuts, lemon juice, and salt to the pan and stir until the peanuts are well coated. Serve warm.

Nigerian Roasted Pepper Chicken

Yield: 8 to 10 Servings

2 (2- to 3-pound) broiler-fryer chickens, cleaned and cut at joints
1 cup peanut oil
1 teaspoon ground red pepper
2 teaspoons salt
1 8-ounce jar pimientos, drained and diced
2 tomatoes, diced
1 large yellow onion, minced

Preheat the oven to 400 degrees. Brush the chicken pieces on both sides with the peanut oil, then season with the ground red pepper and salt. Put the chicken in a large baking dish and sprinkle with the pimiento, tomatoes, and onion. Bake for 45 minutes to 1 hour, until cooked through and browned.

QUICK TIP: *To show your appreciation for a gift of clothing or a toy, take a picture of the baby wearing the clothing or posing with the toy and include it in your thank-you note.*

Chickpea Curry

Yield: 10 to 12 Servings

The Rice Dahomey Style on page 133 is a great side dish for this curry.

    4 tablespoons virgin olive oil or salad oil
 1½ large yellow onions (about 1 pound), diced
    8 celery stalks, ends trimmed, diced
    1 large red bell pepper, stemmed, seeded, and coarsely chopped
    1 large green bell pepper, stemmed, seeded, and coarsely chopped
    8 cloves garlic, minced or pressed
    7 cups chicken broth
 3¼ pounds thin-skinned red potatoes (about 9 medium), scrubbed
        and cut into 1-inch chunks
    4 15½-ounce cans chickpeas or garbanzo beans, drained and rinsed
    2 6-ounce cans tomato paste
    2 tablespoons curry powder
  ½ teaspoon ground red pepper
        Chopped green onion, for garnish (optional)

Heat the oil in a large pot. Reduce the heat to medium. Stir in the onion, celery, red and green bell peppers, and garlic, and cook, stirring, until the vegetables are tender, 7 to 10 minutes. Stir in the broth, potatoes, chickpeas, tomato paste, curry powder, and ground red pepper. Cover and simmer until the potatoes are tender when pierced with a fork, 30 to 40 minutes. Sprinkle with the green onion, if desired.

QUICK TIP: *Set up a "library wish list" for your baby at your local bookstore and send the list and the name of the store with shower invitations.*

West African–Style Spinach with Okra

Yield: 12 Servings

"A child must have a sense of selfhood, a knowledge that he is not here by sufferance, that his forebears contributed to the country and to the world." — John O. Killens, writer

4 10-ounce boxes frozen spinach
3 tablespoons butter or margarine
12 pods fresh okra (2 to 4 inches in length), tips and ends removed, sliced lengthwise
4 tomatoes, peeled and chopped *or* 1 14.5-ounce can peeled tomatoes, chopped
2 medium-sized yellow onions, finely chopped
4 cloves garlic, crushed
4 small slices ginger, finely chopped
   Hot pepper sauce, to taste
2 teaspoons sesame seeds
2 teaspoons salt
2 teaspoons freshly ground black pepper

Cook the frozen spinach according to the package directions. Set aside in a large pan.

Melt the butter in a medium sauté pan. Add the okra, tomatoes, onions, garlic, and ginger, and sauté for 5 to 8 minutes or until the vegetables are tender. Add the vegetable mixture to the cooked spinach. Stir in the hot pepper sauce, sesame seeds, salt, and pepper. Simmer for 5 to 8 minutes to blend the seasonings.

QUICK TIP: Let your guests record their wishes and words of wisdom for the newborn baby in a baby book. It will be fun to read their comments as your child grows up.

Nigerian-Style Munko

Yield: 8 to 10 Servings

This munko recipe from Nigeria is similar to the one that Alex Haley referred to when he described the baby-naming ceremony in Roots, except that the rice is not pounded first and the "dough" is rolled into a ball rather than being patted into a cake before it is fried. Munko is best when served warm.

2 cups cooked white rice, cooled (about ¾ cup uncooked rice)
1 egg, beaten
2 tablespoons unsweetened shredded coconut
2 tablespoons brown sugar
2 tablespoons honey
All-purpose flour
½ cup coconut oil
½ cup peanut oil

Combine the rice, egg, shredded coconut, brown sugar, and honey in a large bowl. Form the mixture into small balls. If the mixture is too loose, add a little flour to bind it; if it is too firm, add a tablespoon or two of water; if it is too sticky, roll the balls in a small amount of flour until lightly dusted.

Place the coconut and peanut oil in a Dutch oven and heat until hot but not smoking, about 375 degrees. Place the rice balls into the hot oil a few at a time and fry until the balls are brown all over, about 3 to 5 minutes. Drain on paper towels.

Frosted Brown-Sugar Spice Cake

Yield: 8 × 12-inch cake

Not only does this fragrant and delicious cake contain sour milk, which is a traditional part of West African celebrations of birth, it also easily serves a crowd.

Spice Cake:
- 1 cup butter or margarine, softened
- 1 cup sugar
- 1¼ cups firmly packed dark brown sugar
- 4 large eggs
- 3 cups all-purpose flour, sifted
- 2 teaspoons baking soda
- 4 teaspoons cocoa powder
- 1 teaspoon salt
- 2 teaspoons ground cinnamon
- 1 teaspoon ground allspice
- ¼ teaspoon ground cloves
- ¼ teaspoon ground nutmeg
- ⅛ teaspoon ground red pepper
- 2 cups buttermilk or sour milk (1 tablespoon vinegar mixed with 1 cup whole milk)

Brown Sugar Frosting:
- 6 tablespoons butter or margarine
- ½ cup light brown sugar
- ¼ cup whole milk

1½ cups confectioners' sugar
¼ teaspoon salt
2 tablespoons light cream
1 teaspoon vanilla

To make the cake, preheat the oven to 350 degrees. Generously grease and flour an 8 × 12-inch cake pan. In a large bowl, using an electric mixer, cream the butter. Gradually add small amounts of the white and brown sugars until the mixture is light and fluffy. One at a time, beat in the eggs. In a separate bowl, sift together the flour, baking soda, cocoa, salt, cinnamon, allspice, cloves, nutmeg, and ground red pepper. Add the flour mixture, a small amount at a time, to the sugar mixture, until well blended. Add the buttermilk and beat until blended, being careful not to overbeat.

Pour the batter into the prepared pan. Bake for 45 to 50 minutes or until a toothpick inserted in the center of the cake comes out clean. Cool the cake for 5 to 10 minutes on a wire rack, then invert onto a serving plate.

To make the frosting, melt the butter or margarine in a small saucepan over low heat. Stir in the brown sugar and milk. Turn the heat to high and bring the mixture to a boil, stirring constantly. Cook for 3 minutes, stirring constantly. Remove the saucepan from the heat. Beat in the confectioners' sugar, salt, cream, and vanilla, beating until the icing is smooth and thick. Allow the icing to cool for 5 to 10 minutes before spreading it over the cake.

Martin Luther King Day Celebration

The Reverend Dr. Martin Luther King, Jr. (1929–1968), became world famous during the Montgomery bus boycott in 1955. Throughout his career he was at the forefront of the nonviolent fight for civil rights and was unafraid to speak out against injustice. His "I Have a Dream" speech, which he delivered on August 28, 1963, at the Lincoln Memorial during the March on Washington, is still one of the most moving orations of our time.

The day of his birth, January 15, is a national holiday in most states as a result of the tireless efforts of his widow, Coretta Scott King. Many communities around the United States pay tribute to Dr. King with a unity march and commemorative services.

Dr. King was also well known for his humor and love of down-home soul food. In her book *My Life With Martin Luther King, Jr.*, Mrs. King fondly recalled some of Dr. King's favorite dishes.

Once, during the summer, when Edythe [Coretta's sister] was there, Martin had said half seriously, "Coretta, how good a cook are you?"

Edythe and I went to his apartment one Sunday afternoon and I cooked my specialty, banana pudding, and Martin's favorite, cabbage smothered in bacon; my sister did creole pork chops. Of course, we had corn bread and tossed salad. Martin and Philip [his roommate] ate it all appreciatively. . . .

Martin always loved southern cooking best . . . He always complained that our cooking was too fattening, yet it was exactly what he loved, and with a plate of greens before him, he never could remember his diet.

I designed the following menu to be served after a community gathering in honor of Dr. King's birthday. Most of the dishes can be prepared well in advance and can be reheated quickly.

MARTIN LUTHER KING DAY CELEBRATION MENU

DRINKS

Lemonade with Frozen Tea Cubes

MAIN DISHES

Creole Pork Chops and Spicy Rice

Pecan Chicken

SIDE DISHES

Cabbage Smothered with Bacon

Savory Green Beans

BREADS AND DESSERTS

Cornmeal Muffins

Old-Fashioned Banana Pudding with Meringue Topping

Lemonade with Frozen Tea Cubes

Yield: About 1 1/2 quarts

"I have a dream that my four little children will one day live in a nation where they will not be judged by the color of their skin but by the content of their character." — Dr. Martin Luther King, Jr., excerpt from address at the March on Washington, August 28, 1963

Frozen Tea Cubes:
- 1 1/2 cups water
- 10 whole cloves
- 2 2-inch-long cinnamon sticks
- 4 Orange Pekoe tea bags
- 1 1/2 cups cold water

Lemonade:
- 4 cups cold water
- Juice of 8 medium lemons (about 1 1/2 cups)
- 1 cup sugar
- Maraschino cherries (optional)
- Lemon or lime slices (optional)

To make the frozen tea cubes, combine the water, cloves, and cinnamon sticks in a medium saucepan. Bring the spice mixture to a boil, then reduce the heat and simmer for 5 minutes. Remove the pan from the heat. Place the tea bags in a large pitcher. Pour the spice mixture over the tea bags. Cover the pitcher with a piece of plastic wrap and let stand 10 minutes. Using a slotted spoon, remove the tea bags and spices. Stir in the cold water. Fill two ice cube trays with the tea mixture and freeze until solid. To make the lemonade, combine the water, lemon juice, and sugar in a large punch bowl and stir until the sugar is dissolved. Place a few of the frozen tea cubes in each glass. Pour the lemonade mixture over the tea cubes and place a cherry in each glass or decorate the rim of each glass with a lemon or lime slice, if desired.

Creole Pork Chops and Spicy Rice

Yield: 4 to 6 Servings

You can prepare the spicy rice the day before if you are pressed for time.

¹/₂ cup vegetable oil
1 cup uncooked white rice
3 cups coarsely chopped tomatoes
1 green bell pepper, diced
1 small yellow onion, chopped
1 clove garlic, minced
1 teaspoon salt
¹/₂ teaspoon freshly ground black pepper
¹/₂ teaspoon hot pepper sauce
6 pork chops, about 1 inch thick
¹/₄ cup water

Heat ¹/₄ cup oil in a large skillet. Add the rice and turn the heat to medium. Sauté the rice, stirring constantly, for 3 to 5 minutes or until lightly browned. Remove the rice from the pan and place it in a medium bowl. Add the tomatoes, green pepper, onion, garlic, ¹/₂ teaspoon salt, ¹/₄ teaspoon pepper, and hot pepper sauce to the rice and set aside.

Sprinkle the pork chops with the remaining ¹/₂ teaspoon of salt and ¹/₄ teaspoon of pepper. Heat the remaining ¹/₄ cup of the oil in the skillet. Brown the pork chops for about 3 minutes on each side. Spoon the rice mixture over the pork chops. Pour in the water, cover, and simmer over low heat for 45 to 55 minutes or until pork chops are cooked through and the rice is tender.

Pecan Chicken

Yield: 4 to 6 Servings

This recipe is a great alternative to fried chicken because it is baked rather than fried in oil. The pecans also add a wonderful flavor to the seasoned biscuit coating.

- 2 cups Bisquick biscuit mix
- $^2/_3$ cup finely chopped pecans
- 4 teaspoons paprika
- 1 teaspoon salt
- 1 teaspoon poultry seasoning
- 1 teaspoon dried sage
- 1 cup evaporated milk
- 2 $2^1/_2$- to 3-pound broiler-fryer chickens, cut into serving pieces
- 1 tablespoon vegetable shortening, for greasing pans
- 1 cup butter or margarine, melted

Preheat the oven to 350 degrees. Combine the biscuit mix, pecans, paprika, salt, poultry seasoning, and sage in a large bowl, and mix well.

Pour the milk in a medium bowl. Dip the chicken in the milk, one piece at a time, then dredge the chicken through the pecan mixture. Repeat the process again, so that all of the chicken pieces have been dipped and dredged twice.

Lightly grease two 13 × 9-inch pans with the vegetable shortening. Place the coated chicken in the pans so that the pieces do not touch each other. Drizzle the melted butter over the chicken pieces. Bake, uncovered, for 1 hour or until the thickest pieces are cooked through.

QUICK TIP: A Tribute to Mrs. Rosa Parks *is a beautiful recording of gospel music by some of the top artists in the field (Shirley Caesar, Yolanda Adams, Vanessa Bell Armstrong, John P. Kee, Sounds of Blackness, and others) as well as Mrs. Parks' own recollections about her life in the struggle. It's a wonderful musical keepsake and will make fabulous background music for your dinner party. Music fills a room and helps your guests relax.*

Cabbage Smothered with Bacon

Yield: 6 Servings

"Courage faces fear and thereby masters it. Cowardice represses fear and is thereby mastered by it." — Dr. Martin Luther King, Jr., from *The Strength to Love* (1963)

> 3 slices bacon, chopped
> 1 small head cabbage, washed and shredded
> 1 large green bell pepper, sliced
> 1 large yellow onion, sliced
> 1 large tomato, peeled and chopped
> 3 stalks celery, cut diagonally into thin slices

Fry the bacon until crisp in a large skillet or Dutch oven. Remove the bacon and set aside, reserving the bacon drippings in the pan as they will add flavor and moisture to the cabbage. Add the cabbage, bell pepper, onion, tomato, and celery to the pan. Raise the heat to high and fry the vegetables, stirring constantly, for 5 to 8 minutes or until the vegetables are crisp-tender. Cover the pan, reduce the heat, and simmer the vegetables for another 5 minutes. Crumble the bacon and sprinkle it over the vegetables.

Savory Green Beans

Yield: 4 Servings

3 tablespoons virgin olive oil
1/2 cup sliced green onions
1 pound green beans, washed and trimmed
1 tablespoon cold water
1 teaspoon salt
1/4 teaspoon freshly ground black pepper
1 1/2 teaspoons red wine vinegar
2 tablespoons finely cut fresh mint leaves (optional)

Heat the oil in a large skillet. Add the green onions and sauté, stirring occasionally, until soft but not brown, 2 to 3 minutes. Stir in the green beans and water, cover, reduce the heat to low, and simmer for 5 minutes. Remove the lid and cook, uncovered, for another 5 to 10 minutes until the beans are crisp-tender. Remove the beans from heat and stir in the salt, pepper, and vinegar. Sprinkle with mint leaves, if desired.

Old-Fashioned Banana Pudding with Meringue Topping

Yield: 8 Servings

This smooth delight is the perfect finale to a soul food meal. Make sure the egg whites are room temperature so the peaks of meringue will be high and light. Keep this dessert away from drafts as a chill will make the meringue shrink.

Pudding:
- 1/2 cup sugar
- 3 tablespoons all-purpose flour
- 1/8 teaspoon salt
- 1 large egg
- 3 eggs, separated (reserve egg whites for the meringue)
- 2 cups whole milk
- 1/2 teaspoon vanilla
- 3 dozen vanilla wafers
- 3 large bananas, peeled, threaded, and sliced

Meringue:
- 3 egg whites (reserved from the pudding)
- 1/4 teaspoon cream of tartar
- 1/4 cup sugar
- 1/4 teaspoon vanilla

To make the pudding, preheat the oven to 350 degrees. Separate the top and bottom parts of a double boiler. Fill the bottom part with water so that the water will come to within ½ inch of the top part. Heat the water to boiling, then reduce the heat to a low simmer. Meanwhile, in the top of the double boiler, combine the sugar, flour, and salt, and mix well. Stir in the whole egg, the 3 egg yolks, and the milk. Mix well. Place the top of the double boiler over the bottom and bring the pudding to a simmer over low heat, stirring almost constantly, for 10 to 15 minutes. When the mixture is smooth and thickened, remove from the heat. Stir in the vanilla.

Spread about ¼ cup of the pudding in an ovenproof casserole dish. Arrange a dozen vanilla wafers on top of the pudding. Place a third of the sliced bananas on top of the wafers. Cover the bananas with pudding and repeat the layering process until all of the pudding, bananas, and wafers have been used.

To make the meringue, place the egg whites in the bowl of a mixer. Beat the egg whites and cream of tartar on high speed for 1 minute until the mixture is foamy. Slowly add the sugar, a tablespoon at a time, beating until stiff peaks form and all of the sugar is dissolved (2 to 4 minutes). Do not underbeat. Beat in the vanilla.

Spoon the meringue over the banana pudding, spreading the meringue to the edges of the casserole dish completely covering all of the pudding. Bake for 12 to 15 minutes or until the meringue is a light golden brown on the peaks.

Cornmeal Muffins

Yield: 12 muffins

Heating the muffin cups allows the shortening to melt and "cook" the batter around the edges of the cup. The muffin is crisp on the outside and moist, hot, and tender on the inside.

2 large eggs
2 cups buttermilk
3 tablespoons melted vegetable shortening
1 teaspoon salt
1 cup cornmeal
1 cup all-purpose flour
1 teaspoon baking soda
3 teaspoons water
1½ teaspoons baking powder

Preheat the oven to 450 degrees. Beat the eggs in a large bowl. Add the milk, shortening, and salt. In a separate bowl, sift together the cornmeal and flour. Add the cornmeal/flour mixture to the egg mixture, beating until smooth. Set the batter aside.

Grease the bottom of 12 muffin cups (about 1½ inches deep). Place the muffin tin in the oven to heat for 3 to 5 minutes. Meanwhile, dissolve the baking soda in the water. Add the baking soda liquid and the baking powder to the batter and mix well. Divide the batter among the heated muffin cups, filling each cup about two-thirds of the way to the top. Bake for 20 to 25 minutes or until the tops of the muffins are golden brown.

February

African-American History Month Buffet

Carter G. Woodson (1875–1950) was the founder of the *Negro History Bulletin*, and the editor of the *Journal of Negro History*. He wrote and edited more books about African-American history than any other historian of his time. Woodson was also one of the founders of the Association for the Study of Negro Life and History (ASNLH, later known as the Association for the Study of Afro-American Life and History) and spearheaded the start of Negro History Week in February 1926. February was chosen because Frederick Douglass's and Abraham Lincoln's birthdays are both celebrated during that month.

Woodson was known in his day as a man with a cause. His determination to preserve African-American history and educate people of all races about the contributions of African-Americans is inspiring. No celebration of African-American History Month would be complete without paying tribute to him.

I designed the menu that follows to reflect the diverse heritage of African-Americans. I also wanted to include recipes from some of the other regions where our ancestors have had a major impact, such as Brazil and the Caribbean.

AFRICAN-AMERICAN HISTORY MONTH BUFFET MENU

DRINKS AND APPETIZERS

Hot Southern Cider

African Fruit Salad with Peanut Butter Dressing

MAIN DISHES

Kenyan Chicken with Coconut Milk

Brazilian Corn and Shrimp Casserole

VEGETABLES

Caribbean New Potatoes

Fresh Vegetables with Sesame Sauce

BREADS AND DESSERTS

Down Home Rolls

Pineapple Upside-Down Cake

Hot Southern Cider

Yield: 1 quart

This old-fashioned favorite is a great way to welcome and warm up your guests.

8 cups apple cider
12 whole cloves
2 cinnamon sticks, broken into pieces
1 teaspoon allspice

Place all of the ingredients in a large saucepan and bring to a boil over high heat, stirring constantly. As soon as the mixture comes to a boil, remove from the heat and strain through a fine sieve. Serve immediately.

QUICK TIP: *African flags make wonderful decorations for your African-American History Month celebration. You can often get flags from embassies or consulates. Since most African flags are composed of simple designs, you can also make them out of felt. If you are planning a large gathering, consider placing miniature flags representing different African countries on each table.*

African Fruit Salad with Peanut Butter Dressing

Yield: 6 Servings

The flavors, textures, and colors in this tropical salad make a pleasing combination. If you can't find a papaya, try substituting two peaches, or a mango.

Fruit Salad:
3   medium seedless navel oranges, peeled and sectioned
2   medium ripe bananas, peeled and sliced
1   ripe papaya, peeled, seeded, and cut into cubes
3   cups pineapple chunks
1 1/2   cups sweetened, shredded coconut

Peanut Butter Dressing:
1/2   cup chunky peanut butter
1/2   cup dark corn syrup
1/2   cup milk

To make the fruit salad, place the oranges, bananas, papaya, pineapple, and shredded coconut in a large bowl and mix gently. Set aside in the refrigerator to chill.

To make the dressing, in a small bowl, stir together the peanut butter and corn syrup until well blended. Add the milk, stirring well. Cover and refrigerate until ready to serve. Just before serving the fruit salad, toss with the dressing.

Kenyan Chicken with Coconut Milk (Kuku Na Nazi)

Yield: 8 to 10 Servings

Coconut milk and coconut cream can be found with the piña colada and daiquiri mixes. Coriander (or cilantro) is usually placed near the fresh parsley in the produce section.

2 2- to 3-pound broiler-fryer chickens, cut into serving pieces
8 cloves garlic, peeled
1 5-inch piece fresh ginger, grated, or 2 tablespoons ground ginger
1 tablespoon curry powder
1/2 teaspoon ground red pepper
2 tablespoons vegetable oil
1 medium-sized yellow onion, sliced
1 cup butter or margarine
1/2 cup chopped fresh coriander (cilantro)
4 cups coconut milk
1 cup coconut cream
   Cooked rice, for serving

Wash the chicken pieces and pat them dry. Grind together the garlic, ginger, curry powder, and ground red pepper in a blender or food processor until fine, 1 to 2 minutes.

Heat the oil in a small skillet. Add the onion and sauté until tender and golden. Add the ground spices, reduce the heat to low, and simmer for 2 to 3 minutes.

Melt the butter in a large Dutch oven over medium heat. Add the chicken to the pot, a few pieces at a time (do not crowd) and cook on all sides until all of the pieces are browned. Add the onion and spice mixture to the chicken pot, turning the chicken pieces to coat them with the spices. Add the coriander and coconut milk and bring the mixture to a boil. Reduce the heat to a simmer, cover the pot tightly, and cook over medium-low heat for 60 to 90 minutes, until the thickest pieces are cooked through and the chicken is tender. Pour the coconut cream over the chicken and remove the pot from the heat. Serve over rice.

Brazilian Corn and Shrimp Casserole

Yield: 6 Servings

2 tablespoons virgin olive oil or butter
1/2 cup chopped yellow onions
1/4 cup chopped green bell pepper
1 pound fresh jumbo shrimp, cleaned and deveined
2 tablespoons chopped fresh parsley
1/4 cup canned tomato sauce
2 tablespoons mild salsa
1 teaspoon salt
1 teaspoon freshly ground black pepper
2 tablespoons all-purpose flour
1 cup whole or 2-percent milk
1 tablespoon vegetable shortening, for greasing the baking dish
2 cups canned cream-style corn
1/2 cup grated Parmesan cheese

Preheat the oven to 375 degrees. Heat the oil in a large skillet. Add the onions and bell pepper and sauté until tender, 3 to 5 minutes. Add the shrimp and parsley and sauté until the shrimp begin to turn pink, 2 to 3 minutes. Stir in the tomato sauce, salsa, salt, and pepper. Reduce the heat to low, cover the skillet, and simmer for 5 minutes. Uncover the skillet and slowly sprinkle the flour over the shrimp mixture. Mix well, then gradually pour in the milk. Raise the heat to medium and cook, uncovered, until the mixture thickens, 3 to 5 minutes. Remove from the heat and allow to cool for a few minutes.

Grease an 8- or 9-inch ovenproof baking dish with the shortening. Spoon the shrimp mixture into the dish. Pour the cream-style corn over the shrimp mixture. Do not stir. Sprinkle the Parmesan cheese on top. Bake for 20 to 30 minutes or until brown.

QUICK TIP: *Records and tapes of the speeches of famous African-Americans like Dr. Martin Luther King, Jr., and Mary McLeod Bethune are often available at public libraries. You may want to play parts of them after dinner.*

Caribbean New Potatoes

Yield: 8 Servings

Jerk seasoning mix contains a variety of spices such as thyme, all-spice, cinnamon, and nutmeg, and gives these potatoes a Caribbean flair.

   1 teaspoon salt
 16 small new potatoes (about 2 pounds), scrubbed and quartered
   2 tablespoons butter or margarine, melted
   2 tablespoons chopped fresh cilantro (coriander)
1¹⁄₂ teaspoons dry jerk seasoning mix

Place the potatoes in a large pot with enough water to cover them. Bring to a boil, cover, and boil until the potatoes are tender, 20 to 25 minutes. Drain the potatoes and place in a large bowl. Sprinkle with the butter, cilantro, and jerk seasoning mix. Toss to coat thoroughly. Serve warm.

Fresh Vegetables with Sesame Sauce

Yield: 6 Servings

"We have a wonderful history behind us . . . It reads like the history of a people in a heroic age . . . We are going back to that beautiful history and it is going to inspire us to greater achievements." — Carter G. Woodson, taken from *Columbus Salley, The Black 100* (1993)

 $^1/_3$ cup butter or margarine
 $^1/_2$ cup canned beef broth
 1 cup peeled and sliced carrots
 1 cup coarsely chopped zucchini
 1 cup cauliflower florets
 1 cup sliced fresh green beans
 1 cup red bell pepper
 1 tablespoon sliced red chile pepper
 $^1/_2$ teaspoon salt

Sesame Sauce:
 1 tablespoon butter or margarine
 2 tablespoons all-purpose flour
 $^1/_2$ cup canned beef broth
 2 tablespoons sesame seeds
 1 teaspoon Dijon mustard
 $^1/_2$ teaspoon salt
 $^1/_2$ cup Parmesan cheese

To prepare the vegetables, melt the butter in a large skillet, and add the beef broth and bring to a boil. Add the carrots, zucchini, cauliflower, green beans, bell pepper, chile pepper, and salt. Cover and cook over high heat until the vegetables are crisp-tender, about 8 to 10 minutes. Do not overcook. Remove the vegetables from the skillet and place in a serving dish.

To make the sauce, melt the butter in a large skillet over low heat. Add the flour, stirring until smooth. Cook, stirring constantly, for about 1 minute. Gradually add the beef broth. Reduce the heat to medium, and cook, stirring constantly, until the sauce is thick and bubbly. Stir in the sesame seeds, mustard, and salt. Continue stirring and reduce the heat to low. Simmer and stir for 1 to 2 minutes. Pour the sesame sauce over the vegetables. Sprinkle with the Parmesan cheese.

Down Home Rolls

Yield: 12 rolls

1 tablespoon vegetable shortening, for greasing the muffin cups
2 cups self-rising flour
1 cup milk
¼ cup mayonnaise

Preheat the oven to 425 degrees. Lightly grease with the vegetable shortening the bottoms of 12 (about 2½-inch) muffin cups. Combine the flour, milk, and mayonnaise in a large bowl and stir until a soft dough has formed. Divide the dough evenly among the muffin cups. Bake until the rolls are browned, about 20 minutes.

QUICK TIP: *Test your guests' knowledge of African-American history with an educational party game. Write out questions about people, places, and events in African-American history. Place the questions in a basket and have each guest select one. This game may be played in teams. Books about African-American history make great prizes.*

Pineapple Upside-Down Cake

Yield: 11 × 14-inch cake

"In the first place, we need to attain economic independence. You may talk about rights and all that sort of thing. The people who own this country will rule this country. They always have done so and they always will." — Carter G. Woodson

Topping:

      4 tablespoons butter or margarine
    ½ cup firmly packed brown sugar
      1 30-ounce can pineapple slices, drained
    10 maraschino cherries
    ½ cup chopped pecans

Cake Batter:

    2 cups cake flour
    2 tablespoons baking powder
    ¼ teaspoon salt
    ¼ cup vegetable shortening
    1 cup sugar
    1 large egg, beaten
    1 teaspoon vanilla
    ¾ cup milk

To make the topping, grease an 11 × 14-inch pan with 1 tablespoon of the butter. Sprinkle the brown sugar in the pan. Place a layer of pineapple slices on top of the sugar. Place a cherry in the center of each slice. Dot the remaining butter in and around the pineapple slices. Sprinkle with the pecans.

To make the cake batter, sift together the flour, baking powder, and salt in a medium bowl. Cream the shortening in a large bowl. Gradually add the sugar and beat until fluffy. Add the egg and vanilla and mix well. Alternately add the flour mixture and milk in small amounts, stirring until the batter is smooth. Pour the batter over the fruit. Bake for 50 to 60 minutes until the cake is brown on top and a toothpick inserted in the center of the cake comes out clean. Cool the cake in the pan. Place a serving platter on top of the cake pan and turn upside down to release the cake onto the platter.

African-Style Engagement Dinner for Two

I love romance, and Valentine's Day is one of my favorite holidays. Although my husband tells me he loves me all year long, it sounds even better when I hear it on Valentine's Day.

If you've chosen Valentine's Day as the day to propose or make a strong commitment, why not incorporate some African traditions into the evening? In Ghana, the courtship and proposal process is called "making custom."

You may want to "make custom" by presenting your love with a beautiful necklace made of gold or Venetian glass beads, a symbol of a pending marriage in many parts of Africa. A necklace engraved with African Nubian khamitic symbols, such as the ankh, which means eternal life and love and respect of life, or the pyramid (the mer-khut), which means power, strength, and permanence, makes a wonderful gift. The necklace not only becomes a special keepsake, it will be in keeping with the way many of our ancestors proposed marriage. Choosing the rings can be an event you both participate in at a later time.

In some African communities it is traditional to share a kola nut with your love and your families and friends when you become engaged. According to this custom, the prospective groom and his family approach the prospective bride's family about marriage. If the woman's family accepts the proposal, then she is offered a kola nut. If she accepts the nut, the groom's family gives the bride's family a small amount of money. The woman breaks open the nut and shares a small piece of it with the prospective groom. Then the rest of the nut is shared with the family.

Kola nuts are imported, and are available in some gourmet and herb shops. Because of their high caffeine content, these round, bitter, red-orange nuts are often used alone, or in combination with other herbs, as a stimulant.

AFRICAN-STYLE ENGAGEMENT DINNER FOR TWO MENU

DRINKS AND APPETIZERS

Suggested Wines

Cucumber Love Boats with Sour Cream Dressing

MAIN DISH

Steak and Shrimp

SIDE DISHES

Easy Broccoli Parmesan

Twice-Baked Potatoes

DESSERT

Chocolate Passion Pie

Suggested Wines

Price does not always indicate quality when it comes to wine. An inexpensive white wine like chardonnay may be served before dinner, and red cabernet sauvignon with dinner. You can pop open champagne if your proposal is accepted. Good luck!

White Wines
California chardonnay
French montrachet

Red Wines
California cabernet sauvignon
Bordeaux Cabernet Sauvignon

Cucumber Love Boats
with Sour Cream Dressing

Yield: 2 Servings

1 large cucumber
1 stalk celery, shredded
1/2 medium carrot, shredded
1/2 teaspoon salt

Sour Cream Dressing:
1/2 cup sour cream
1/2 teaspoon distilled white vinegar
1/2 teaspoon sugar
1/2 teaspoon freshly ground black pepper
1/4 teaspoon dried dill weed
Shredded lettuce
Cherry tomatoes, cut in half (optional), for garnish

Slice the cucumber lengthwise and scoop out the seeds. In a small bowl, combine the celery, the carrot, and salt. Divide the mixture evenly between the cucumber halves.

To make the sour cream dressing, in a small bowl, combine the sour cream, vinegar, sugar, pepper, and dill. Spoon the sour cream mixture on top of the cucumber halves. Place the cucumber halves on a bed of shredded lettuce on salad plates. Garnish with tomatoes.

QUICK TIP: *Why send just one Valentine's Day card? For extra romance, send one valentine a day, starting on February 1. The fourteen cards are a great buildup to your dinner date, and are fun to receive.*

Steak and Shrimp

Yield: 2 Servings

"To love is to make one's heart a swinging door." — Howard Thurman from Morehouse Student Oration (1948)

 2 tablespoons virgin olive oil
 2 cloves garlic, thinly sliced
 6 jumbo shrimp, peeled and deveined, tails intact
 3 tablespoons Chablis or other dry white wine
 2 beef tenderloin steaks, 1 inch thick
 1 teaspoon salt
 1 teaspoon freshly ground black pepper
    Parsley sprigs, for garnish

Preheat the broiler. Heat the oil in a small skillet over medium heat. Add the garlic and sauté for 1 to 2 minutes. Add the shrimp and cook, stirring, until they turn pink, 2 to 3 minutes. Remove the shrimp from the skillet. Add the wine to the skillet, stirring well, then return the shrimp to the skillet, stirring to coat each one with the sauce. Remove the skillet from the heat, cover, and set aside.

Place the steaks in a shallow pan for broiling and season both sides with salt and pepper. Place the steaks about 6 inches from the heat source and broil 4 to 5 minutes on each side, or a few minutes longer if you prefer your steak medium-well or well-done. Do not overcook. Place the steaks on 2 serving plates. Place the shrimp to one side of the steak and cover the shrimp with the wine sauce. Garnish with the parsley sprigs.

Easy Broccoli Parmesan

Yield: 4 Servings

"For news of the heart, ask the face." — Hausa proverb

> 1 **10-ounce package frozen broccoli spears**
> 1 **tablespoon virgin olive oil**
> 1 **teaspoon salt**
> 1 **teaspoon freshly ground black pepper**
> 1/2 **teaspoon red wine vinegar**
> 1/4 **teaspoon sugar**
> 1/4 **cup grated Parmesan cheese**

Cook the broccoli spears according to the package directions and set aside in a small pan. Combine the oil, salt, pepper, vinegar, and sugar in a small bowl. Pour the oil mixture over the broccoli. Cook over low heat for 1 to 2 minutes to blend the seasonings. Remove the broccoli spears from the pan and place in a serving bowl. Sprinkle the broccoli with the Parmesan cheese.

Twice-Baked Potatoes

Yield: 2 Servings

2   medium baking potatoes, scrubbed and rubbed with vegetable oil
$1/2$ cup cream-style cottage cheese
2   tablespoons butter or margarine, softened
1   tablespoon mayonnaise
1   tablespoon snipped chives
$1/4$ teaspoon salt
$1/8$ teaspoon freshly ground black pepper
$1/2$ teaspoon sweet paprika
2   tablespoons shredded Cheddar cheese

Preheat the oven to 400 degrees. Prick the potatoes with a fork so they will release steam as they cook. Bake in the oven for 1 hour or in the microwave on high for 8 to 10 minutes or until cooked through. Set the oven at 375 degrees.

When the potatoes are cool enough to handle, cut them in half lengthwise. Being careful to leave the shells intact, scoop out the pulp and mash it in a medium bowl. Add the cottage cheese, butter, mayonnaise, chives, salt, and pepper and mix well. Stuff the shells with the potato mixture.

Place the stuffed potato halves in a shallow baking pan and sprinkle with the paprika and cheese. Bake for 15 to 20 minutes or until the cheese is melted and potatoes are thoroughly heated.

QUICK TIP: *Sprinkle a few drops of your signature cologne on the light bulbs around the house. This makes the house smell wonderful and invokes pleasant thoughts about you.*

Chocolate Passion Pie

Yield: One 9-inch Pie

This cool, creamy, rich dessert is pure passion in a pie shell. It's the perfect finish for a romantic meal.

- $1\frac{1}{2}$ cups ground almonds
- 3 tablespoons sugar
- 2 tablespoons butter or margarine, softened
- 1 pint chocolate ice cream, softened
- 1 pint vanilla ice cream, softened
- 1 8-ounce can chocolate sauce
- Slivered almonds, for garnish

Preheat the oven to 400 degrees. Combine the almonds, sugar, and margarine in a large bowl. Firmly and evenly press the nut mixture into the bottom and sides of a ungreased 9-inch pie plate. Bake the pie shell for 6 to 8 minutes or until crust turns light brown. Cool.

Scoop the chocolate ice cream into the cooled pie shell. Smooth and top with the vanilla ice cream. Freeze until firm, about 4 hours. Remove from the freezer 10 to 15 minutes before serving. Drizzle each serving with chocolate syrup and sprinkle with slivered almonds.

March

Women in History Month— Sisters' Rejuvenation Brunch

What would we do without our sisters? Whether they share our genes and our bloodline or our jeans and our blouses, we need the support system only another woman can give. Why not treat your sisters and friends to brunch and a relaxing day designed to soothe both body and soul in March, the month that celebrates women?

Gather a group of your women friends together and take turns giving each other facials, manicures, and pedicures. Use large, disposable aluminum roasting pans for foot soaks. You may use fresh milk, milk on the verge of going bad, or some powdered milk, mixing it into the water to soften the skin and revitalize the feet. Sprinkle some cornstarch in your shoes before you slip them back on. Cornstarch absorbs moisture and odor and makes your feet feel more comfortable.

Have your friends scrub their nails with soap and a nail brush then soak their nails in small bowls of warm olive oil for about 10 minutes. Massage the excess oil into one another's cuticles and knuckles, one finger at a time, then massage the hands. It's great for your nails and very relaxing.

Make a facial and foot scrub out of cornmeal and mayonnaise, just like our grandmothers did. Simply mix together 1 ½ cups cornmeal with 1 cup mayonnaise and massage the mixture lightly on the face, elbows, knees, and feet. Rinse with lukewarm water and pat dry. To make an astringent, combine the juice of two lemons with some ice-cold mineral water. Use a cotton ball to dab it on the skin.

The rejuvenation party will help everyone to cleanse their pores and souls and slough off old skin and worries. You might also listen to music or books on tape, watch weepy "tearjerkers" or read selections from your favorite authors aloud. Use the party as a time to tell each one of your sister friends what she means to you and how much you appreciate her love and support. This is a party that will make everyone feel better inside and out.

WOMEN IN HISTORY MONTH— SISTERS' REJUVENATION BRUNCH MENU

DRINKS AND APPETIZERS

Sunrise Punch

Moroccan Almond Milk

Fruit-stuffed Apples

MAIN DISHES

Vegetable and Egg Scramble

Zanzibar Sesame Pancakes

Liberian Pineapple Nut Bread

Sunrise Punch

Yield: 8 Servings

This punch has an attractive rose-colored hue.

¹/₄ cup grenadine syrup
1¹/₂ quarts chilled grapefruit juice

   Just before serving, pour 1¹/₂ teaspoons grenadine into eight 8- to 10-ounce glasses. Hold the teaspoon in one of the glasses, right side up and about ¹/₂ inch above the grenadine, and slowly and carefully pour in ³/₄ cup of the grapefruit juice. The juice should trickle over the grenadine without actually mixing with it. Repeat with the remaining glasses.

QUICK TIP: *Ask everyone to wear a hat, an African head wrap, or crown to brunch. It's lots of fun and a great icebreaker for guests who don't know each other.*

Moroccan Almond Milk

Yield: 8 4-ounce cups

The zest of citrus fruits such as oranges, lemons, and limes is the colored peel containing the fruit's oil and flavor but not the underlying bitter white pith. You can remove the peel with a paring knife or a lemon zester.

1 12-ounce package whole almonds, toasted and finely ground (see Note)
1 cup firmly packed brown sugar
1 cup water
4 cups milk
2 tablespoons orange zest, grated

Combine the almonds and sugar in a small bowl. Stir in ½ cup of the water and set aside for 30 minutes. When ready, pour the almond mixture into a blender and blend on low speed. Slowly add the remaining ½ cup water and blend until smooth. Set aside for another 30 minutes. Warm the milk slightly in a medium saucepan; do not let it boil. Add the orange zest and the almond mixture and stir until smooth.

NOTE: To toast seeds and nuts (whole or in pieces), arrange them in a single layer on a baking sheet and bake at 350 degrees for about 5 minutes, shaking the baking sheet occasionally, until golden brown. Toasting seeds and nuts brings out their flavor and aroma. Watch them carefully as they cook quickly and burn easily.

QUICK TIP: *Make your own unique invitations for your rejuvenation brunch by cutting the shape of an African queen's crown out of construction paper, then use the same design for your place cards.*

Fruit-stuffed Apples

Yield: 6 Servings

"All African-American women may not have rocking chairs, but we have each other." — Opal Palmer Adisa

    6 **large Granny Smith apples**
    1 **cup canned juice-packed fruit salad (juice drained and reserved)**
    2 **teaspoons sugar**
    1 **teaspoon apple pie spice**

Preheat the oven to 375 degrees. Core the apples, leaving the bottoms solid. Do not peel. Place the apples, open ends up, in a small nonstick roasting pan. Combine the fruit salad, sugar, and apple pie spice in a small bowl, then spoon into the hollowed-out apples. Pour the reserved juice over and around the apples. Bake for 45 minutes, basting occasionally, until the apples are just barely tender.

QUICK TIP: *Light some incense and scented candles and place them around the room. The fragrance is relaxing as well as pleasant.*

Vegetable and Egg Scramble

Yield: 6 Servings

To save time, the night before your gathering, boil the potatoes (un-peeled). The next day peel and dice them. If you peel the potatoes in advance, they will turn brown.

8 eggs
6 tablespoons water
2 tablespoons minced yellow onion
$1\frac{1}{2}$ teaspoons salt
$\frac{1}{2}$ cup butter or margarine
2 cups diced tomatoes
2 cups diced cooked potatoes
2 cups diced zucchini

Combine the eggs, water, onion, and salt in a small bowl and beat until fluffy.

Melt the butter in a large skillet over medium heat. Add the tomatoes, potatoes, and zucchini, and spread into an even layer. Pour the egg mixture on top. As the mixture begins to set on the bottom and sides, gently lift portions of it with a spatula so that the thin, un-cooked egg can flow to the bottom of the pan and cook. Cook until the eggs are thickened throughout but are still moist, 3 to 5 minutes.

QUICK TIP: *Rent a yoga videotape and have your guests do the in-troductory stretches. Yoga limbers and relaxes the muscles and pro-vokes a feeling of well-being.*

Zanzibar Sesame Pancakes

Yield: 10 pancakes

Zanzibar is a corruption of an Arab word that means "the coast of the Blacks." This recipe is from that area. The toasted sesame seeds in these pancakes give them a slightly crunchy texture.

       1 **teaspoon dried yeast**
      2/3 **cup warm water**
       1 **teaspoon sugar**
       1 **cup all-purpose flour**
      2/3 **cup milk**
      1/2 **cup vegetable oil**
       3 **tablespoons sesame seeds, toasted (see Note on page 93)**
          Jam or jelly, for serving (optional)

Dissolve the yeast in the warm water in a small bowl. Stir in the sugar and put the uncovered mixture in a warm place until it starts to foam, about 5 minutes. If it does not foam, the yeast is too old. Discard the mixture and start the process over again with a fresh package of yeast.

Sift the flour into a large bowl. Make a well in the center of the flour with a large spoon. Stir the yeast mixture into the well. Slowly add the milk, stirring constantly, and continue to stir until the batter is smooth and thick and runs slowly from the spoon. If the batter is too thick, add warm water 1 tablespoon at a time.

Heat 1 tablespoon of the oil in a skillet over medium heat. Spoon in batter until it spreads to form a pancake about the size of a saucer. Cook until the pancake is golden brown on the bottom, about 1 minute.

Sprinkle a few drops of oil on the pancake, then turn it over to cook on the other side. Sprinkle the top with a few of the toasted sesame seeds. Repeat the process with the remaining batter, adding oil as necessary to prevent the pancakes from sticking. Serve warm with jam or jelly, if desired.

QUICK TIP: *Play some soothing music and have your guests sit quietly for a few minutes with their eyes closed. Then have everyone inhale and exhale deeply about ten times. This is a relaxing way to start off your party.*

Liberian Pineapple Nut Bread

Yield: One 9½-inch loaf

This is a great recipe to prepare a day ahead of time. The bread tastes even better the second day, buttered, toasted, and spread with jam.

- 1 tablespoon vegetable shortening, for greasing the pan
- 2½ cups all-purpose flour
- 1 tablespoon baking powder
- 1 teaspoon baking soda
- 1 teaspoon salt
- 1 cup toasted wheat bran
- 2 eggs, beaten
- ¾ cup canned crushed pineapple, drained and juice reserved
- 1 cup canned pineapple juice
- ½ cup chopped walnuts

Preheat the oven to 350 degrees.

Grease a 9½-inch loaf pan with the vegetable shortening. Sift the flour, baking powder, baking soda, and salt into a large bowl. Stir in the bran. Add the eggs, crushed pineapple, canned pineapple juice, and walnuts and combine thoroughly. If the dough is too stiff or won't bind, add the reserved pineapple juice 1 tablespoon at a time until it is smooth. Spread the batter into the prepared loaf pan. Bake for 1 hour or until a toothpick or cake tester inserted into the center of the loaf comes out clean.

April

Traditional Easter Dinner

To me, April means spring, moving Easter church services, revival both in nature and in spirit, children in their Sunday best, and family dinners. I enjoy Easter egg hunts almost as much as my grandbaby Anysa does. Each year, my sister and I take turns buying matching frilly dresses for my niece Marcy and Anysa. I enjoy seeing them transformed into beautiful black princesses on Easter Sunday morning and taking them to church.

Easter morning church services have always been soul-stirring occasions, although the message has remained the same for hundreds of years. On Easter morning the scriptures about resurrection, forgiveness, and renewal are even more special.

I love traditional family dinners and Easter dinner is one of my favorites. If you're planning an Easter dinner for your family, you may want to mix traditional dishes with a few new recipes. You might start a brand new Easter tradition.

TRADITIONAL EASTER DINNER MENU

DRINKS AND APPETIZERS

Pink Punch

Deviled Eggs

MAIN DISH

Lemon-roasted Leg of Lamb with Wild Rice

SIDE DISHES

Corn and Cucumbers

Sour Cream Green Beans

BREADS AND DESSERTS

Sesame-Cheese Bread

Strawberry Pie

Pink Punch

Yield: About 2 gallons

"I feel a real kinship with God, and that's what has helped me pull out of the problems I've faced. Anybody who has kept up with my career knows that I've had my share of problems and trouble, but look at me today ... Through the years, no matter how much success I achieved, I never lost my faith in God." — Aretha Franklin, singer

- 3 6-ounce cans frozen pink-lemonade concentrate, partly thawed
- 3 6-ounce cans frozen orange juice concentrate
- 4 quarts ginger ale
- 4 quarts soda water
- 3 8-ounce packages frozen sliced strawberries, partly thawed

Combine the pink lemonade, orange juice, ginger ale, soda water, and strawberries in a large punch bowl and stir until all of the ingredients are well blended. Serve over ice.

Deviled Eggs

Yield: 8 Servings

Sprinkle paprika around the rim of the serving plate to add a decorative touch to this dish.

8 hard-cooked eggs
$1/2$ ounce packaged cream cheese, softened
2 tablespoons light mayonnaise
2 teaspoons sweet pickle relish
1 teaspoon white distilled vinegar
1 teaspoon freshly squeezed lemon juice
1 teaspoon mustard
$1/8$ teaspoon sugar
$1/8$ teaspoon garlic salt
$1/8$ teaspoon curry powder
Sweet paprika

Slice the eggs in half lengthwise. Remove the yolks and place them in a medium bowl. Mash the yolks with a fork, then stir in the cream cheese until well blended. Mix in the mayonnaise, relish, vinegar, lemon juice, mustard, sugar, garlic salt, and curry powder. Spoon the yolk mixture into the egg white halves. Sprinkle with paprika just before serving.

Lemon-roasted Leg of Lamb
with Wild Rice

Yield: 6 Servings

Do not remove the paperlike covering, called the fell, from the lamb. The lamb will cook faster, keep its shape, and be juicier with the fell intact.

1	3- to 4-pound leg of lamb
1/2	cup distilled white vinegar
1/2	cup water
	Juice of 1 lemon
	Zest of 1/2 lemon
1 1/2	teaspoons dried mustard
2 1/2	teaspoons salt
1	teaspoon freshly ground black pepper
	Wild Rice, for serving (recipe follows)

Preheat the oven to 300 degrees. Place the leg of lamb, fat side up, in a shallow roasting pan with a rack. Using a sharp paring knife, make small 1-inch deep cuts, spaced about 1 inch apart all over the top of the lamb. Combine the vinegar, water, freshly squeezed lemon juice and zest, mustard, 1 teaspoon of the salt, and the pepper in a small saucepan and bring to a boil. Pour the vinegar mixture over the lamb. Bake the lamb for 1 1/2 hours, basting frequently and sprinkling with the remaining 1 1/2 teaspoons salt during the last 30 minutes of cooking. Remove the lamb from the oven and allow it to sit for 20 to 25 minutes for easier carving. Carve into thin slices and serve surrounded by wild rice. Fill a gravy boat with the remaining marinade to serve at the table.

Wild Rice

Yield: 8 Servings

To wash the wild rice, place it in a wire strainer and run cold water through it. You can assemble this dish the day before then bake it while the lamb is "resting" and waiting to be carved.

- 1/4 cup butter or margarine, melted
- 1 cup chopped green bell pepper
- 1 cup fresh button mushrooms, sliced
- 1/2 cup chopped green onions, tops included
- 1 cup uncooked wild rice
- 1/2 cup uncooked white rice
- 4 10.5-ounce cans beef broth
- 1 cup whipping cream
- 1 teaspoon salt
- 1/4 teaspoon freshly ground black pepper
- 1 teaspoon vegetable shortening, for greasing casserole dish

Preheat the oven to 350 degrees. Melt the butter in a Dutch oven over medium heat. Add the green pepper, mushrooms, and green onions and sauté until tender but not brown, about 3 to 4 minutes. Remove the vegetables from the Dutch oven and set aside.

Combine both kinds of rice, the beef broth, whipping cream, salt, and pepper in the Dutch oven. Set the heat on high and bring the rice to a boil, stirring once or twice. Reduce the heat to low, cover, and simmer for 40 to 50 minutes, checking after 30 minutes to make sure that the rice is not sticking to the pan; add 1/4 cup hot water if it is. Combine the cooked rice with the sauteed vegetables. Grease a 3-quart casserole dish with the vegetable shortening. Pour the rice mixture into the dish and bake for 20 to 25 minutes.

Corn and Cucumbers

Yield: 6 Servings

2 medium cucumbers, peeled and thinly sliced
½ medium-sized yellow onion, thinly sliced
1 17-ounce can whole kernel corn, drained
½ cup distilled white vinegar
2 tablespoons sugar
2 tablespoons water
1 teaspoon dried dill weed
¼ teaspoon freshly ground black pepper
   Dash of ground red pepper
1 teaspoon paprika

Combine the cucumbers, onion, corn, vinegar, sugar, water, dill weed, black pepper, and ground red pepper in a medium serving bowl. Mix well. Sprinkle with paprika. Chill and serve.

Sour Cream Green Beans

Yield: 6 Servings

"There has been a crucifixion in our nation, but here in this spring season as we see the blossoms and smell the fresh air we know that the Resurrection will shortly appear." — Comment of Reverend Ralph Abernathy after the assassination of Dr. Martin Luther King, Jr.

   1/2 cup butter or margarine
     1 yellow onion, thinly sliced
     2 10-ounce packages frozen green beans, thawed and drained
     1 cup dairy sour cream
   1/4 cup all-purpose flour
1 1/2 teaspoons salt
   1/4 teaspoon freshly ground black pepper
     1 cup (4 ounces) shredded sharp Cheddar cheese
     1 cup soft bread crumbs

Preheat the oven to 350 degrees. Grease a 1 1/2-quart casserole dish. Melt 1/4 cup of the butter in a small skillet. Add the onion and sauté until tender. Combine the green beans, onion, sour cream, flour, salt, and pepper in the prepared casserole dish, mixing lightly. Sprinkle with the cheese. Melt the remaining 1/4 cup butter in the skillet over medium heat. Remove the pan from the heat and mix in the bread crumbs, tossing until the crumbs are coated with butter. Top the green bean casserole with the bread crumbs. Bake for 25 minutes or until crumbs are a golden brown.

Sesame-Cheese Bread

Yield: 1 loaf

"My hope for my children must be that they respond to the still, small voice of God in their own hearts." — Rev. Andrew Young

3¾   cups Bisquick biscuit mix
1¼   cups (5 ounces) shredded sharp Cheddar cheese
1¼   cups milk
  1   egg
½   teaspoon dry mustard
  1   tablespoon sesame seeds

Preheat the oven to 350 degrees. Grease a 9-inch loaf pan. Combine the biscuit mix, cheese, milk, egg, and dry mustard in a large bowl and beat on low speed with an electric mixer until all of the ingredients are moistened. Increase the speed to medium and beat for an additional minute. Spoon the batter into the prepared pan and sprinkle with the sesame seeds. Bake for 1 hour 10 minutes or until a toothpick inserted in the center comes out clean. Remove the bread from the pan immediately. Cool on a wire rack.

Strawberry Pie

Yield: 9-inch pie

"I want to see how life can triumph." — Romare Bearden, artist

- 4 **cups fresh strawberries**
- 2 **3-ounce packages cream cheese, at room temperature**
- 1 **9-inch Party Pastry, baked (recipe follows)**
- ³/₄ **cup sugar**
- ¹/₃ **cup cornstarch**
- ¹/₄ **teaspoon salt**
- ¹/₄ **cup water**
- 1 **cup heavy cream, whipped, for serving**

Wash and stem the strawberries. Cut 2 cups of the strawberries in half and set aside. Using an electric mixer set on medium speed, beat the cream cheese and 4 of the whole strawberries in a large bowl until fluffy. Spread the mixture over the bottom and sides of the pie shell. Combine the sugar, cornstarch, and salt in a medium saucepan. Gradually add the water and, stirring constantly, cook for 2 minutes over low heat. Add the strawberry halves to the saucepan and simmer gently over low heat for 5 minutes or until the mixture is clear and thickens. Cool. Fold in the remaining whole strawberries and pour the filling into the pie shell. Chill. Serve topped with whipped cream.

Party Pastry

Yield: 4 9-inch pastry shells

"I don't know what the future may hold, but I know who holds the future." — Rev. Ralph Abernathy

> 4 cups all-purpose flour
> 1 tablespoon sugar
> 2 teaspoons salt
> 1³/₄ cups vegetable shortening
> 1 egg, beaten
> ¹/₂ cup cold water
> 1 tablespoon distilled white vinegar
> Additional flour for rolling out dough

Preheat the oven to 400 degrees. Combine the 4 cups of flour, the sugar, and salt in a large bowl. Using a pastry blender or fork, blend in the shortening until the mixture looks coarse like cornmeal. Combine the egg, water, and vinegar in a small bowl, then stir this mixture into the flour mixture, combining gently until a soft dough forms.

Divide the dough into 4 equal parts, wrap tightly in plastic wrap, and chill for 1 hour or freeze for future use. Using a lightly floured rolling pin, roll out one ball of the chilled dough on a floured board. Place in a 9-inch pie pan, and trim off excess pastry along the edges. Pinch or flute the edges of the crust as desired. Prick the bottom and sides of the crust with a fork and bake for 10 to 12 minutes or until golden brown.

Blue Monday Party

If you need an "attitude adjustment" why not start the week with a Blue Monday party in honor of Billie Holiday? By the time you laugh with your friends and listen to the soulful sounds only Lady Day can wring out of a song, you'll be ready for anything.

Billie Holiday was born on April 7, 1915, in Baltimore, Maryland, to teenage parents. Her real name was Eleonora Fagan, but her father called her Bill because she was such a tomboy. She changed her name to Billie, after silent-film star Billie Dove.

She grew up poor and often neglected, but Billie Holiday, influenced by Bessie Smith and Louis Armstrong, began making her musical mark at an early age. Singing with the bands of Count Basie, Duke Ellington, Fletcher Henderson, and Benny Goodman made her internationally famous.

Bad relationships, alcohol, and drugs toppled her from the heights of fame and caused her death at age 44. Despite it all, Billie Holiday's ability to turn simple words into powerful songs full of heartfelt emotion lives on. There's nothing like listening to Lady Day to soothe the soul.

Jazz and blues are African-American gifts to the music world. A party centered around and celebrating our own special brand of music is in keeping with our ancestors' long love affair with music and dance.

BLUE MONDAY PARTY MENU

DRINKS AND APPETIZERS

Vineyard Crush

Blue Cheese Ball and Crackers

MAIN DISHES

Spicy Fried Catfish

Honey Chicken Wings

VEGETABLES

Baked Scalloped Corn

Brussels Sprouts in Beer

Bluesy Zucchini

BREADS AND DESSERTS

Aunt Florine's Jalapeño Cornbread

Easy Fruit Cobbler

Vineyard Crush

Yield: 1 quart

"Oh the blues ain't nothing but a good woman feeling bad."
— Recorded by Georgia White, blueswoman, 1938

  1 24-ounce bottle grape juice, chilled
  1 cup orange juice, chilled
  1/4 cup lemon juice, chilled
  1/2 cup sugar
  1 quart ginger ale, chilled

Combine the grape juice, orange juice, lemon juice, and sugar in a large pitcher or punch bowl and stir until the sugar has dissolved. Just before serving, stir in the ginger ale. Serve over ice.

Blue Cheese Ball and Crackers

Yield: 10 Servings

This cheese ball is best when the seasonings have had a few days to mingle. Covered tightly, it will keep in the refrigerator for several weeks.

> 2 8-ounce packages cream cheese, softened
> 8 ounces blue cheese, softened
> 4 tablespoons butter or margarine
> 1/2 cup chopped black olives
> 2 tablespoons minced fresh parsley
> 1 tablespoon snipped fresh chives
> 3 tablespoons chopped nuts
> Assorted crackers

Combine the cream cheese, blue cheese, and the butter in a large bowl and stir until the ingredients are well blended. Add the olives, parsley, and chives, mix well, and form into a ball. Place the chopped nuts on a plate. Roll the cheese ball in the nuts until well coated. Wrap in plastic wrap and refrigerate until ready to serve. Surround the cheese ball with your favorite crackers and serve.

Spicy Fried Catfish

Yield: 12 Servings

"I've been told that nobody sings the word 'hunger' like I do. Or the word 'love.' Maybe I remember what those words are all about."
— Billie Holiday

> 12   catfish fillets, halved
> 1   cup spicy Dijon mustard
> 1¼   cups white cornmeal
> ½   teaspoon salt
> 1 to 1½   teaspoons ground red pepper
> ½   teaspoon freshly ground black pepper
>   Vegetable oil, for frying
>   Parsley sprigs, lemon wedges, and purple onion rings
>   (optional), for garnish

Lightly brush the fillets with half the mustard. Put the cornmeal, salt, and red and black pepper in a plastic bag and shake until blended. Drop the catfish into the cornmeal mixture one piece at a time and shake until the fish is completely coated. Brush the fillets with the remaining mustard and coat again with the cornmeal mixture. Fill a 3- to 4-inch-deep skillet halfway with oil. Heat the oil until hot but not smoking, about 330 degrees. Carefully place the fillets in the skillet and fry until they float to the top and are golden brown. Transfer the fried fillets to a paper towel–lined plate to drain. Serve hot. Garnish with parsley sprigs, lemon wedges, and purple onion rings, if desired.

Honey Chicken Wings

Yield: 6 Servings

"God has blessed you when he lets you believe in somebody."
— Recorded by Billie Holiday

        1 cup honey
        1 cup teriyaki sauce
        1 cup yellow mustard
        1 cup butter or margarine, melted
        2 teaspoons curry powder
    2 to 3 pounds chicken wings, cleaned
        1 tablespoon vegetable oil, for greasing pan

Preheat the oven to 350 degrees. Combine the honey, teriyaki sauce, mustard, butter, and curry powder in a large bowl. Dip each piece of chicken into the honey mixture until well coated.

Grease a large roasting pan with the vegetable oil. Place the chicken wings in the pan, wing tips up. Pour any remaining sauce over the chicken wings. Bake for about 1 hour, basting occasionally.

Baked Scalloped Corn

Yield: 6 Servings

1 17-ounce can whole-kernel corn, drained
1 17-ounce can cream-style corn
1/4 cup milk
1/4 cup crushed Ritz brand crackers
1/4 cup chopped yellow onion
2 eggs, beaten
1 2-ounce jar chopped pimiento, drained
1/4 teaspoon salt
1/4 teaspoon freshly ground black pepper
2 tablespoons grated Parmesan cheese
1 tablespoon butter or margarine

Preheat the oven to 350 degrees. Grease a 9-inch casserole dish. Combine the whole-kernel and cream-style corn, the milk, crackers, onion, eggs, pimiento, salt, and pepper in a large bowl. Pour the mixture into the prepared casserole dish and sprinkle the top with the cheese. Dot with butter. Bake, uncovered, for 40 to 45 minutes or until the center is almost set. Let stand 5 minutes before serving.

Brussels Sprouts in Beer

Yield: 4 to 6 Servings

"Somebody once said we never know what is enough until we know what's more than enough." — Recorded by Billie Holiday

1   **pound fresh brussels sprouts, or 2 10-ounce packages frozen brussels sprouts**
1   **12-ounce can beer**
2   **tablespoons butter or margarine, melted**
¹⁄₂ **teaspoon salt**

Combine the brussels sprouts and beer in a large saucepan. Bring to a boil, then cover, reduce the heat to a simmer, and cook for 10 to 12 minutes or until tender. Drain the brussels sprouts, then add the butter and salt and stir to coat.

Bluesy Zucchini

Yield: 4 to 6 Servings

"Everybody in the world has the blues ..." — John Lee Hooker, musician

$1/3$ cup butter or margarine
3 cups zucchini slices
1 medium-sized yellow onion, sliced
1 teaspoon dried oregano leaves, crushed
$1/2$ teaspoon salt
$1/4$ teaspoon freshly ground black pepper
1 medium tomato, cut into wedges

Melt the butter in a medium skillet. Add the zucchini and onion to the pan, sprinkle with the oregano, salt, and pepper, and sauté for 8 to 10 minutes or until the vegetables are tender. Add the tomatoes and cook for another 5 minutes.

Aunt Florine's Jalapeño Cornbread

Yield: 12 Servings

My Aunt Florine loaned this recipe to a coworker, who in turn gave it to her friend Bennie Hannon. Years later Bennie Hannon met my uncle, Ricky Davis, at a party. Bennie had never met my Aunt Florine, but my Uncle Ricky recognized her cornbread recipe as soon as he tasted it. It's a small world when you love food.

1 15-ounce can cream-style corn
1 cup yellow cornmeal
1 cup whole milk
2 eggs
1/2 teaspoon salt
1/2 teaspoon baking soda
1 pound mild pork sausage
8 ounces Cheddar cheese
1 large onion, chopped
2 medium jalapeño peppers, chopped
1 tablespoon vegetable shortening, for greasing pan

Preheat the oven to 350 degrees. Combine the corn, cornmeal, milk, eggs, salt, and baking soda in a large bowl. In a small skillet, cook the sausage, using a fork to break the meat into small pieces. Stir the sausage and the sausage grease into the cornmeal batter. Stir in the cheese, onion, and peppers. Grease an 8-inch square baking pan with the vegetable shortening. Pour the batter into the baking pan and bake for 45 minutes. If a tester inserted in the center of the bread comes out clean, remove it from the oven. If not, cook the cornbread for 10 minutes longer and retest for doneness.

Easy Fruit Cobbler

Yield: 6 Servings

"You can be dressed up to your boobies in white satin, with garde-nias in your hair and no sugar cane for miles, but you can still be working on a plantation." — Recorded by Billie Holiday

    1 cup each apples and peaches, peeled, pitted, and cored
    1 cup cherries, pitted
1³/₄ cup sugar
    2 tablespoons cornstarch
 ¹/₄ teaspoon freshly squeezed lemon juice
    1 tablespoon butter or margarine
    1 cup sifted all-purpose flour
    2 teaspoons baking powder
 ¹/₂ teaspoon salt
    2 teaspoons vegetable shortening
 ¹/₂ cup milk
 ¹/₂ teaspoon cinnamon
 ¹/₂ teaspoon nutmeg
    1 teaspoon sugar
     Whipped cream or ice cream, for serving

Preheat the oven to 375 degrees. Mix together the apples, peaches, and cherries in a large bowl with the sugar, cornstarch, and lemon juice, then transfer to a 9-inch square baking dish, heaping the fruit high in the center so that it will support the crust. Dot the fruit with the butter. Combine the flour, baking powder, and salt in a medium bowl. Using a fork or pastry blender, cut the shortening into the flour mixture until crumbly. Stir in the milk to make a soft dough. On a lightly floured cutting board, roll out the dough to a ½-inch thick square. Place the dough over the mound of fruit. Cut air vents in the top and seal the edges securely. Combine the cinnamon, nutmeg, and sugar in a small bowl, then sprinkle on top of the dough. Bake for 35 minutes or until brown and bubbly. Serve with whipped cream or ice cream.

May

National Malcolm X Day Dinner

Malcolm X (El Hajj Malik El-Shabazz, 1925–1965) was born Malcolm Little in Omaha, Nebraska. He was molded by a strong, black nationalist father and a proud, well-educated mother. After his father's murder, his mother struggled to hold the family together. Money was scarce and she had to be creative with the scant food that they had. In the book *The Autobiography of Malcolm X*, he says:

> We all loved chicken. That was one dish there was no argument with my father about. One thing in particular that I remember made me feel grateful toward my mother was that one day I went and asked her for my own garden, and she did let me have my own little plot . . . I especially loved to grow peas. I was proud when we had them on the table . . . Our mother knew, I guess dozens of ways to cook things with bread and out of bread . . . Bread pudding, sometimes with raisins in it . . . But there were times when there wasn't even a nickel and we would be so hungry we were dizzy.

Although the odds were against him, he overcame hardship, the destruction of his family, misdirection, and prison to become one of the most influential leaders of the civil rights movement. His life was changed after a conversion to Islam. After his pilgrimage to Mecca, he split with the Nation of Islam and founded the radically different Organization of Afro-American Unity, which, unlike the Nation of Islam, included all races.

Malcolm X had the unique ability to lead and to inspire people because of his absolute devotion to his cause. He did not always want to be in the limelight, although he projected an aura that attracted attention. He was not covetous of money or power, and because he was fearless, he gave others courage. He was assassinated on February 21, 1965.

Tributes to the memory of Malcolm X are held in many cities around the United States. Symposia, commemorative marches, speeches, poster contests, rap contests, prison outreach programs, and other celebrations in Malcolm's memory are held on his birthday, May 19. Organization for the day begins on the anniversary of his death with the hanging of posters and banners urging support for National Malcolm X Day.

I think it only fitting that the recipes for a Malcolm X Memorial Day Dinner include dishes from the South, Africa, and the Moslem culture Malcolm embraced before his death.

NATIONAL MALCOLM X DAY DINNER MENU

DRINKS AND APPETIZERS

Southern Citrus Tea

Ethiopian Lentil Salad

MAIN DISH

Congo Chicken Moambe

Rice Dahomey Style

VEGETABLES

Porkless Mixed Greens

Southern Green Peas

DESSERT

Bread Pudding

Southern Citrus Tea

Yield: 8 Servings

6 cups brewed tea (made with 4 tea bags)
1 cup apple juice
1 cup orange juice
1 cup pineapple juice
3 tablespoons freshly squeezed lemon juice
1 stick cinnamon

Combine the tea, apple, orange, pineapple, and lemon juices, and the cinnamon stick in a large pitcher, mixing well to combine. Refrigerate and serve over ice.

Ethiopian Lentil Salad

Yield: 8 Servings

The Ethiopian name for this unusual and spicy salad is Yemiser Selatta. *Allow the salad to marinate at room temperature to allow the spices to mingle.*

    2½ cups (about 1 pound) dried lentils
    6 tablespoons red wine vinegar
    ¼ cup vegetable oil
    1½ teaspoons salt
    ½ teaspoon freshly ground black pepper
    8 large shallots, peeled and halved lengthwise
    1 fresh hot green chili, stemmed, seeded, and julienned

Wash the lentils in a sieve under cold running water. Bring to a boil a medium pot of water to which you have added a pinch of salt. Add the lentils. The water should cover them by 2 or 3 inches. Partly cover the pot. Simmer for 25 to 30 minutes or until the lentils are crisp-tender. Drain the lentils in a sieve, cool them under cold running water, then drain them again and set aside.

Combine the vinegar, oil, salt, and pepper in a deep bowl and whisk until well-blended. Stir in the lentils, shallots, and green chili until they are well coated. Marinate the salad at room temperature for at least 30 minutes, stirring gently from time to time.

Congo Chicken Moambe

Yield: 8 Servings

Chicken Moambe, of which there are many variations, has been called the National Dish of the Congo. This is the version I like best because the seasonings blend so well. This recipe is easy to double or triple as needed.

> 2   3-pound broiler-fryer chickens, disjointed
> 2   teaspoons salt
> 1   teaspoon ground red pepper
> 3   tablespoons butter
> 2   yellow onions, minced
> 2½   cups canned tomato sauce
> ½   teaspoon nutmeg
> 1   cup peanut butter

Season the chicken with the salt and ground red pepper. Place the seasoned chicken pieces in a large pot. Cover the pieces with water, bring to a boil, cover, reduce heat to a simmer and cook until tender, 45 minutes to 1 hour.

Melt the butter in a large saucepan. Add the onions and sauté until golden brown, about 5 minutes. Add the tomato sauce and nutmeg and simmer uncovered for about 5 minutes. Remove a cup of the tomato sauce and reserve. Add the chicken and simmer over low heat, covered, for about 5 minutes.

In a medium bowl, combine the reserved tomato sauce with the peanut butter until smooth and slightly liquified. Add the peanut butter mixture to the pan to thicken the sauce and simmer uncovered for another 10 minutes.

Rice Dahomey Style

Yield: 4 Servings

This dish is a simpler version of a recipe from Africa. The olives and broth are a flavorful addition to the rice.

2 cups canned chicken broth
1 cup uncooked Uncle Ben's converted rice
$1/2$ teaspoon salt
$1/4$ teaspoon freshly ground black pepper
1 bay leaf
$1/4$ cup chopped pimiento-stuffed olives (optional)

Bring the chicken broth to a boil in a large pot. Reduce the heat to low and add the rice, salt, pepper, and bay leaf. Cover and cook until the broth is absorbed and the rice is fluffy, about 15 minutes. Remove the bay leaf. Mix in the olives, if desired.

Porkless Mixed Greens

Yield: 6 Servings

I substituted smoked turkey for the traditional pork in this recipe to stay in keeping with the Muslim dietary law that forbids the consumption of pork.

        1½ pounds collard greens
        1½ pounds kale
         1 tablespoon salt
         1 1½-pound package smoked turkey wings
        ¼ cup vegetable oil
         1 clove garlic, chopped
        ¼ teaspoon sugar
            Ground red pepper, to taste

Cut the tough stems and yellow leaves from the greens and discard. Gently rub the leaves with your fingers under warm running water to remove the grit, then cut the leaves into small pieces. Fill the sink with warm water and add the salt. Let the greens soak in the warm, salted water for 10 minutes, then rinse with cool water and shake off excess; do not dry the greens.

Put the turkey, greens, oil, garlic, sugar, and ground red pepper in a Dutch oven or heavy pot. Do not add water. Cover and cook over low heat for 60 to 90 minutes, stirring every 15 minutes until the greens are tender.

Southern Green Peas

Yield: 6 Servings

Although Thomas Jefferson receives much of the credit for introducing the so-called "English" or green pea to American cuisine, it was actually his slave chef, James Hemings, who created the recipes and did the cooking. When Jefferson was ambassador to France, Hemings accompanied him and studied the art of French cooking. Hemings then combined his African-American culinary heritage with his French training. Hemings often used vanilla, almonds, and raisins in his dishes, and prepared such dishes as macaroni, cornbread stuffing, waffles, and ice cream for Jefferson's dinner guests. His creations were unique at that time and quickly became standards of American cuisine.

- 1/2 cup canned chicken stock
- 3 cups shelled fresh or frozen green peas
- 4 green onions, trimmed of roots and outside layers
- 5 tablespoons butter or margarine
- 1 tablespoon chopped fresh thyme
- 1 teaspoon salt
- 1 teaspoon freshly ground black pepper
- 1/4 teaspoon sugar

Bring the chicken stock to a boil in a large pot over high heat. Carefully stir in the peas, green onions, butter, and thyme. Bring the mixture to a boil, cover, and cook for 6 to 8 minutes or until the peas are slightly tender. Stir in the salt, pepper, and sugar.

Bread Pudding

Yield: 6 Servings

Nothing went to waste in those old-fashioned kitchens. Stale or evaporated bread is used in this recipe because the dry bread soaks the flavors of the pudding like a sponge without becoming mushy. The bread was dressed up with apples and turned into a tasty desert. Apples such as Baldwin, Golden Delicious, Ida Red, Rome Beauty, and Winesap are good varieties for this recipe.

    1 tablespoon freshly squeezed lemon juice
$^1\!/_2$ cup firmly packed brown sugar
    4 sweet apples, peeled, cored, and cubed
$^3\!/_4$ cup milk, scalded
    2 eggs, beaten
$^1\!/_4$ cup granulated sugar
    2 tablespoons butter or margarine, melted
$^1\!/_2$ teaspoon nutmeg
$^1\!/_2$ teaspoon vanilla
$^1\!/_2$ cup raisins
    8 slices white bread
    1 cup bread crumbs

Combine the freshly squeezed lemon juice and $^1\!/_4$ cup of the brown sugar in a medium mixing bowl. Add the apples and stir to coat. Refrigerate for 1 hour.

Preheat the oven to 450 degrees. Grease a 1-quart casserole or 9-inch square baking pan. Combine the remaining $^1\!/_4$ cup brown sugar, the milk, eggs, granulated sugar, butter, nutmeg, vanilla, and raisins in a large bowl. Tear the bread into pieces and add it to the bowl. Mix well, mashing the bread. Add the apples and all the sugary liquid that has accumulated in the bowl with them to the bread mixture. Mix well.

Pour the batter into the prepared pan and sprinkle with the bread crumbs. Cover with aluminum foil and bake for 30 minutes. Uncover and bake 5 minutes longer or until a knife inserted into the center comes out clean.

Memorial Day Dinner
on the Grounds Picnic

My mother often tells me stories about gathering with the other members of the small church she attended in the backwoods of Oklahoma and Kansas for the Memorial Day Dinner on the Grounds picnic. Memorial Day, which began after the Civil War, was originally called Decoration Day and was set aside as a time to honor those who died in the war and tend to their graves.

For many African-Americans, the holiday became a time to gather with other church members to clean the church cemetery and pay tribute to family members who had died. The pastor would offer up a prayer and then the men would clean and weed the graves. After the graves were clean, the women and children would decorate them with homemade crèpe paper flowers in brilliant colors. Some families would plant flowering bushes or trees near the headstones. As in African tradition, the ancestors, although dead and gone, were still lovingly cared for by the members of the family. Once the graveyard was decorated, dinner was served.

Sometimes dinner was eaten on the ground picnic-style or a plank table set on hobby horses was used. Each mother would bring a sparkling-clean white sheet to use as a tablecloth. Then, as if by magic, the table would be covered with some of the finest food in Oklahoma! After eating for a while with one's own family, everyone would move around to sample the leftovers at other tables. Each cook had a delicious "specialty" dish; my mother's was her Raisin-Pecan Pie. After dinner the adults had a rare chance to visit, while the children played ring games, hide-and-seek, and stickball.

Reviving the Memorial Day Dinner on the Grounds tradition is important, especially for African-Americans, because so much of our family history was lost because of slavery. Graveyards hold a wealth of information about family history. Studying tombstones is like reading a brief history of a person's life. Usually the date of birth and death are listed, as well as the maiden names of married women. Some tombstones list the person's occupation, and the names of all the children in the family, while others describe how the person died. Sometimes a picture of the person is embedded in the tombstone.

If you know where your ancestors are buried, visit the site. Take pictures, both close-up shots and wide-angle views of the entire site. Cemeteries are often built over or moved without notice. The pictures provide a visual record and also show landmarks that will help other visitors find the grave site. You may also want to take a rubbing of the stone as a keepsake. You'll need several large, thin sheets of paper (the thinner the paper, the better the image is after the rubbing) and either a wax crayon from which you have removed the paper covering, a large soft lead pencil (similar to the type small children use), or a piece of artist's charcoal. You will also need a fixative spray to keep your rubbing from getting smudged or wearing off when you store it and a whisk broom to clean off the surface dirt on the headstones so that your rubbing will be clear.

To do the rubbing, whisk off any dirt from the stone. Place the paper over the part you want to copy. Holding the paper firmly, rub the crayon, pencil, or charcoal back and forth until the words or image appear and darken. To preserve your rubbing, follow the directions on the can of fixative spray. Be careful when make a rubbing of soft stone or old wood. These can be worn down if rubbed too much.

MEMORIAL DAY DINNER ON THE GROUNDS PICNIC MENU

DRINKS AND APPETIZERS

Coconut Cream Cooler

Banana-Pineapple Salad

MAIN DISH SANDWICHES AND SPREADS

Beef-stuffed Sandwich Loaf

Curried Chicken Spread

Shrimp Spread

Vegetarian Sandwich Spread

DESSERT

Angeline's Raisin-Pecan Pie

Coconut Cream Cooler

Yield: 1 gallon

"When you kill the ancestor you kill yourself." — Toni Morrison, author

> 1 46-ounce can pineapple juice
> 1 15.5-ounce can cream of coconut
> 1 12-ounce can frozen orange juice concentrate, thawed
> 7½ cups water
> 1 teaspoon almond extract

Combine the pineapple juice, cream of coconut, orange juice concentrate, water, and almond extract in a large container. Stir well. Serve over ice.

Banana-Pineapple Salad

Yield: 4 Servings

Peanuts add a satisfying crunch to this sweet salad.

> 2 tablespoons freshly squeezed lemon juice
> 2 tablespoons honey
> ¼ teaspoon cinnamon
> 2 bananas, peeled, threaded, and sliced diagonally
> 1 14-ounce can pineapple chunks, with juice
> ½ cup chopped unsalted peanuts

Combine the lemon juice, honey, and cinnamon in a small bowl. Combine the bananas, pineapple, and peanuts in a medium bowl. Drizzle the honey mixture over the fruit, tossing lightly. Chill.

Beef-stuffed Sandwich Loaf

Yield: 4 Servings

This sandwich tastes good hot or at room temperature. It's perfect for a picnic basket. To keep it warm longer, first wrap the hot sandwich in heavy-duty aluminum foil. Make sure the shiny side of the foil is against the sandwich. Then wrap again in several layers of newspaper. If desired, you can substitute ground turkey for the beef in this recipe.

     8 ounces lean ground beef
  1¹/₂ teaspoons virgin olive oil
     1 large yellow onion, chopped
     1 carrot, grated
   ¹/₄ cup chopped fresh parsley
     1 tablespoon mild salsa
     1 teaspoons salt
   ¹/₄ teaspoon freshly ground black pepper
   ¹/₄ teaspoon sweet paprika
     1 loaf unsliced thick-crusted bread (such as rye, French, or
        sourdough)
     1 medium-sized yellow onion, grated
   ¹/₂ cup water

Preheat the oven to 325 degrees. Combine the beef, olive oil, and onion in a skillet and cook over medium heat until the beef is lighty browned. Add the carrot, parsley, salsa, salt, pepper, and paprika and cook for 5 minutes, stirring occasionally. Drain, place in medium bowl and set aside. (Alternatively, to microwave the beef, crumble it into a 3-quart microwavable casserole. Mix in the olive oil, onion, carrot, parsley, salsa, salt, pepper, and paprika. Cover loosely and microwave on high for 5 minutes. Break up the meat and stir the mixture with a fork. Cover and microwave until the meat has browned, 6 to 8 minutes longer.) Cut a slice from one end of the bread and set aside. Pull out the soft center of the bread. Mix the bread from the center with the meat mixture. Add the grated onion and water. Mix well. Stuff the meat mixture back into the hollowed-out bread loaf. Put the cut slice back on and fasten it with a toothpick. Bake the loaf for 15 minutes. Slice to serve.

QUICK TIP: *Skip the chips. For a delicious crunch, pack your picnic basket with carrot sticks or baby carrots, celery, radish slices, or cucumber slices and serve them with your sandwiches.*

Curried Chicken Spread

Yield: 4 Servings

1 cup cut-up cooked chicken or 1 (5½-ounce) can boned chicken,
 chopped
1 medium-sized yellow onion, chopped
½ small green bell pepper, chopped
½ cup chopped salted peanuts
½ cup light mayonnaise or salad dressing
1 tablespoon freshly squeezed lemon juice
¾ teaspoon curry powder

Combine the chicken, onion, bell pepper, peanuts, mayonnaise, lemon juice, and curry powder in a medium bowl and chill. Spread on sandwich bread.

Shrimp Spread

Yield: 4 Servings

"Bringing the gifts that my ancestors gave, I am the dream and the hope of the slave. I rise, I rise, I rise." — Maya Angelou, poet, author

  8 ounces medium shrimp, cleaned and cooked
$^1/_2$ cup butter or margarine, softened
$^1/_2$ teaspoon salt
$^1/_2$ teaspoon freshly ground black pepper
  1 tablespoon freshly squeezed lemon juice
$^1/_4$ teaspoon Tabasco sauce
$^1/_4$ teaspoon Worcestershire sauce

Combine the shrimp, butter, salt, pepper, lemon juice, Tabasco, and Worcestershire sauces in a blender and process until smooth. Chill. Spread on sandwich bread or crackers.

Vegetarian Sandwich Spread

Yield: 4 Servings

"My great-grandma told my grandma the part she lived through that my grandmama didn't live through and my grandmama told my mama what they both lived through and my mama told me what they all lived through and we suppose to pass it down like that from generation to generation so we'd never forget."—from the book *Eva's Man* by Gayl Jones

<blockquote>

1 cup chopped raisins

$1/2$ cup bean sprouts

$1/2$ cup shredded cabbage

$1/2$ cup shredded carrots

$1/2$ cup chopped apple

$1/4$ cup low-fat salad dressing

1 tablespoon freshly squeezed lemon juice

</blockquote>

Combine the raisins, bean sprouts, cabbage, carrots, apple, salad dressing, and lemon juice in a medium bowl until well blended. Chill. Spoon on sandwich bread or crackers.

Angeline's Raisin-Pecan Pie

Yield: 9-inch pie

My mother's recipe for raisin-pecan pie is unique, creamy, and delicious. She has always been a creative person and a wonderful cook.

- 1½ cups raisins
- ½ cup butter or margarine
- 1¼ cups sugar
- 2 eggs
- 1 cup pecan halves
- 1 teaspoon ground nutmeg
- 1 teaspoon ground cinnamon
- 1 teaspoon vanilla
- 1 9-inch Party Pastry, unbaked (page 111)

Preheat the oven to 350 degrees. Put the raisins in a saucepan, cover with water, and bring to a boil. Boil for 2 to 3 minutes until plump. Drain and set aside.

Cream the butter and sugar in a medium bowl until fluffy. Add the eggs and combine well. Mix in the raisins, pecans, nutmeg, cinnamon, and vanilla. Pour the mixture into the unbaked pie shell. Bake until golden brown and set, 35 to 45 minutes.

June

Juneteenth Caribbean-Style Dinner

On June 19, 1865, Major General Gordon Granger stood on the balcony of Ashton Villa in Galveston, Texas, and read a special order from President Abraham Lincoln:

> The people of Texas are informed that in accordance with a proclamation from the Executive of the United States all slaves are free. This involves an absolute equality of rights and rights of property between former masters and slaves, and the connection heretofore existing between them becomes that between employer and free laborer. The freedmen are advised to remain at their present homes and work for wages. They are informed that they will not be allowed to collect at military posts, and they will not be supported in idleness, either there or elsewhere.

Instantly, June 19, or Juneteenth for short, became a day of celebration and family reunions in Texas.

President Lincoln signed the Emancipation Proclamation on January 1, 1863. It seems hard to believe that it took two-and-a-half years for the news to reach Texas. An old folktale explains that

President Lincoln sent the news from Washington by a Union soldier who rode all the way on a slow-moving mule. According to some historians, many slave owners in Texas were aware of the Emancipation Proclamation but refused to tell their slaves about it.

HOW TO MAKE A FIRE

Always start your fire at least 40 minutes before you plan to start cooking. Clean the grill rack with soap, water, and a wire brush, removing any burned-on food or soot, then set it aside to dry. To keep food from sticking, rub a cool grill rack with salad oil or spray with a nonstick cooking spray. Never spray a grill rack with oil once you've started a fire.

Make a drip pan out of aluminum foil if the grill is not equipped with one, and place the drip pan in the center of the grill. If you use charcoal lighter fluid to start your fire, don't cover the grill until you are ready to cook. Otherwise, the charcoal lighter fluid will not have a chance to burn off and will give the food an unpleasant taste. In addition, the fire may go out or flare up when the cover is lifted. Never spray charcoal lighter fluid on an open flame.

The best items for making a fire are twisted pieces of newspaper and mesquite charcoal for better flavor. Mound the charcoal on top of the paper in a pyramid shape and light the newspaper. Do not dump the charcoal into the grill as the coal dust interferes with the fire. Open the bottom dampers of the grill to fan the flames.

No matter what type of charcoal you use, the coals will probably take 8 to 10 minutes to light and 25 to 30 minutes to get red-hot. Opening the damper on the grill and mounding the charcoal close together will make the fire hotter. Spreading the coals apart, and partially closing the dampers will cool it down. Closing the dampers altogether will help put the fire out. Adjust the dampers according to the type of food.

Steaks, pork, veal chops, hamburgers, liver, boneless chicken breasts, shrimp, and fish steaks and fillets need a very hot fire. Meats that require a long cooking time also need additional coals to maintain heat. To add coals,

Juneteenth was celebrated in Texas until the late 1960s and early 1970s. The civil rights movement seemed to overshadow the holiday. But in the late 1970s, Juneteenth became a popular holiday again, and the tradition began to spread beyond the borders of Texas.

IN THE GRILL

place 10 to 12 briquets around the outer edge of the hot coals. Move these coals to the center of the grill with a long pair of tongs as needed in the cooking progress to maintain an even temperature.

Game birds, seafood, vegetables and bread require a cooler fire, so spread out the coals. Fatty foods, such as pork ribs, chicken halves, brisket, and duck, and foods that take a long time to cook, such as turkey, should be cooked over a drip pan with coals on either side.

Adding damp wood chips, such as oak, apple, hickory, or mesquite, during the last stages of the grilling process imbues the food with extra flavor. Read the instructions on the package carefully. They must soak for a while to absorb enough water to smoke properly.

When using wooden skewers, soak them in water for 15 minutes before threading the food on them and placing them on the grill. This will keep them from burning. Always place cooked foods on a clean dish. Never use the dish that held the raw meat, poultry, or seafood without washing it with soap and hot water first. The bacteria from the raw meat can cause serious illnesses.

Always keep a bucket of water on hand when grilling foods in case of a flash fire. A spray bottle is also handy for applying small amounts of water on the coals to control flare-ups from dripping grease. Keep the grill away from low-hanging eaves, dry grass, flammable material, and the sack of charcoal. When you are done cooking drown the coals with water until there is no more steam; coals left unattended can reignite hours after you've stopped cooking. To be on the safe side, always place ashes in a metal container when cleaning out the grill.

JUNETEENTH CARIBBEAN-STYLE DINNER MENU

DRINKS

Strawberry-Lemonade Punch

MAIN DISHES

Spicy West Indies Fish

Jamaican Jerk Pork Chops

VEGETABLES

Honey-Grilled Vegetables

Calypso Corn

BREADS AND DESSERTS

Grilled Garlic Bread

No-Bake Brownies

Strawberry-Lemonade Punch

Yield: 4½ quarts

"There was plenty of 'so-good' (a 'so-good' tasting strawberry punch) and soda water, and ice-cold watermelon for later on. The feast lasted until late in the afternoon." — Anna Pearl Barrett describing a Juneteenth celebration, 80 years after Emancipation

      2 cups boiling water
    ½ cup sugar
      2 teaspoons peppermint extract
      2 (10-ounce) packages frozen strawberries, thawed
      5 cups cold water
      2 6-ounce cans frozen pink lemonade concentrate, thawed

Combine the boiling water, sugar, and peppermint flavoring in a large container and stir until the sugar is dissolved. Let the sugar mixture stand for 5 minutes. Add the strawberries, stirring well. Using a big spoon, press the strawberry mixture through a large strainer into a pitcher or punch bowl until nothing is left in the strainer except for the strawberry pulp. Discard the pulp. Stir in the cold water and lemonade. Mix until well blended.

Spicy West Indies Fish

Yield: 8 Servings

You can use any good-quality white fish in this dish, but trout and flounder are my favorites. You can also do most of the preparation ahead of time and take the marinated fish in an ice chest to the park to grill. Fish cooks quickly on the grill so you'll have a spicy feast ready in just a few minutes.

> 4 pounds filleted snapper
> 1½ cups freshly squeezed lime juice
> 1 tablespoon curry powder
> 1 tablespoon ground cumin
> 1 tablespoon paprika
> 1 tablespoon allspice
> 1 tablespoon powdered ginger
> 1 tablespoon salt
> 1 tablespoon freshly ground black pepper
> 1½ teaspoons cayenne pepper
> Virgin olive oil or cooking spray

Soak the fish in lime juice for 30 minutes in a glass pan or non-corrosive dish. Remove the fish, reserving the juice. Combine the curry powder, cumin, paprika, allspice, ginger, salt, black pepper, and cayenne pepper in a small bowl and stir until well blended. Place each fish fillet on an individual sheet of aluminum foil. Coat each fillet with the spice mixture. Sprinkle a tablespoon of the lime juice over each piece of fish. Wrap each fillet tightly in the foil.

Remove the rack from the grill and lightly oil it with vegetable oil where the fish will be placed. Make a fire in the grill and heat the coals until they become somewhat white with ash. Place the fish packets on the grill and cook for 5 minutes. Turn the fish packets and cook for another 3 minutes. Open a packet to see if the fish is done. The flesh should be opaque and the skin should pull away from the flesh; flakiness is usually a sign of overcooking.

Jamaican Jerk Pork Chops

Yield: 6 Servings

Jerk is the Caribbean method of marinating meats before barbecuing, and is one of the most popular dishes in Jamaica. The technique for making jerk was created by the Arawaks, the first settlers of the Caribbean islands, and developed into a mouthwatering island tradition by the Maroons, who were runaway Caribbean slaves. The combined methods of spicing and smoking the meat preserved it, which was necessary in the remote places where the Maroons took refuge. The vegetables and spices used in jerk can easily be found in the wild on the islands and in our own tamer grocery stores.

^{1}/$_3$ cup vegetable oil
^{1}/$_3$ cup distilled white vinegar
    4 green onions, chopped
    2 cloves garlic, chopped
    1 Scotch bonnet chile, seeded and minced
    3 bay leaves
    3 peppercorns
1-inch piece cinnamon, crushed
    1 tablespoon ground allspice
    1 teaspoon freshly ground black pepper
^{1}/$_2$ teaspoon ground nutmeg
    3 pounds pork chops, about 1 inch thick

Combine the oil and vinegar in a small bowl. Stir in the green onions, garlic, chile, bay leaves, peppercorns, cinnamon stick, allspice, pepper, and nutmeg.

Trim any excess fat from the pork chops. Place the pork chops in a baking pan and pour the spice mixture over them, coating each chop well. Place the chops in the refrigerator to marinate overnight.

Allow the chops to come to room temperature before grilling. Heat the grill until the coals are somewhat white with ash; the flame should be low. Place the chops on the grill and cover with the lid. Grill for 5 to 10 minutes per side, until the chops are no longer pink in the center.

Honey-Grilled Vegetables

Yield: 6 Servings

If you prefer, you can microwave the potatoes or any of the other vegetables on high for 3 to 4 minutes, instead of boiling in water, before grilling. This will reduce the time they need to cook on the grill without sacrificing the smoky flavor or appealing grill marks.

12	small red potatoes, halved
1/4	cup honey
3	tablespoons dry white wine
1	clove garlic, minced
1	teaspoon dried thyme, crushed
1/2	teaspoon salt
1/2	teaspoon freshly ground black pepper
2	zucchini, cut into quarters
1	medium eggplant, sliced 1/2-inch thick
1	green bell pepper, cut vertically into eighths
1	red bell pepper, cut vertically into eighths
1	large yellow onion, sliced into 1/2-inch thick pieces

Cover the potatoes with water in a large Dutch oven. Bring to a boil, then reduce the heat to a simmer and cook on low for 5 minutes, until the potatoes are tender but firm. Drain.

Combine the honey, wine, garlic, thyme, salt, and pepper in a small bowl and mix well. Brush the vegetables with the honey marinade. Place the vegetables on skewers, if desired.

Lightly oil the grill rack with vegetable oil. Heat the grill until the coals are somewhat gray with ash; the flame should be low.

Place the skewered or loose potatoes, zucchini, eggplant, green pepper, red pepper, and onion directly on the greased grill. Grill the vegetables for about 10 minutes, brushing them with the honey marinade every few minutes and turning them after 5 minutes.

Calypso Corn

Yield: 6 Servings

The colors of the ingredients used in this dish are festive and delicious.

- 1 10-ounce package frozen corn kernels, thawed
- 2 15-ounce cans black beans or white kidney beans, drained and rinsed
- 1 large red bell pepper, stemmed, seeded, and diced
- 1 small fresh jalapeño chili, stemmed, seeded, and minced
- 1/2 cup firmly packed chopped fresh coriander (cilantro)
- 1/4 cup freshly squeezed lime juice
- 2 tablespoons vegetable oil
- 1 teaspoon sugar
- 1 teaspoon salt
- 1 teaspoon freshly ground black pepper

Combine the corn, beans, bell pepper, jalapeño, cilantro, lime juice, oil, sugar, salt, and pepper in a large bowl. Taste and adjust seasonings. Cover and chill 1 hour or overnight to combine flavors.

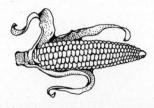

Grilled Garlic Bread

Yield: 8 Servings

- 1/4 cup virgin olive oil
- 1 clove garlic, mashed and diced
- 1 teaspoon dried basil
- 1/2 teaspoon dried oregano
- 8 slices (3/4 inch thick) French bread
- 1 cup shredded mozzarella cheese

Preheat the grill until the coals are somewhat gray with ash; the flame should be low.

Meanwhile, combine the olive oil, garlic, basil, and oregano in a small bowl. Brush both sides of the bread with the olive oil mixture and sprinkle one side of the bread with the cheese. When the coals are ready, place the bread, cheese side up, on the grill. Cover and cook the bread until the cheese melts and the underside of the bread is toasted, 1 to 2 minutes. Serve warm.

No-Bake Brownies

Yield: 32 squares

This recipe is especially appealing during very warm weather, when you don't want to heat up the house by turning on the oven.

2   12-ounce packages semisweet chocolate bits
1   cup unsalted butter
5   cups graham cracker crumbs
2   cups walnuts, chopped
2   14-ounce cans sweetened condensed milk
2   teaspoons vanilla

Fill the bottom pan of a double boiler so that the water will come to within $1/2$ inch of the top pan. Heat the water to boiling, then reduce the heat to a low simmer. Place the chocolate and butter in the top pan over the hot water. Cook over low heat, stirring occasionally, until melted. Alternatively, melt the chocolate and butter in microwave oven set on low (50 percent), stirring once every minute until the mixture is smooth.

Place the graham cracker crumbs, walnuts, condensed milk, and vanilla in a large bowl. Stir in the melted chocolate and butter and mix until well blended and thick. Spread the batter into 2 9-inch baking pans. Let stand at room temperature for 3 hours. Cut the brownies into squares and wrap with plastic wrap. Store brownies in a cool place.

Jumping the Broom
Rehearsal Dinner

The rehearsal dinner is traditionally given by the groom's parents the night before the wedding, following the rehearsal, but friends or other relatives may want to host the dinner instead. My mom prepared a simple, buffet-style dinner after my brother's wedding rehearsal. Everyone was there, from his college friends to members of the wedding party, some of whom I was meeting for the first time. It was a casual, fun evening, and the relaxed atmosphere allowed everyone to get acquainted easily and calm down before the big day.

"Jumping the broom" is a major step, and if you are a bundle of nerves, maybe my story will give you courage. My husband, Michael, and I were acquainted all of six weeks before we got married. I was eighteen and he was twenty. More than twenty-three years have gone by. Now, he works twenty feet away from me everyday. I still think he's sexy and I still enjoy his company.

Obviously, we grew up together, but more importantly, we've grown together. He patiently ate some of the worst meals in the western world until I learned how to cook. He married a girl and helped to shape me into a woman. He supports my dreams and schemes no matter how wild they may sound to others. When I wanted to become a writer, he worked two part-time jobs and a full-time job so I could devote myself to learning my craft and getting published. Now it's his turn to stretch his creative wings and I'm behind him one hundred percent.

If you've been blessed to find your soul mate, never take that blessing for granted. Weddings are sometimes a whirlpool of stress but remember, it's the marriage, not the wedding, that is most important.

The suggested rehearsal dinner menu is simply delicious. Almost everything can be prepared ahead of time and reheated or assembled quickly. Good luck and congratulations!

JUMPING THE BROOM REHEARSAL DINNER MENU

DRINK AND APPETIZERS

Pat's Wedding Punch

Gala Salmon Roll

Festive Fruit Salad

MAIN DISHES

Marinated Chicken with Bananas

SALADS AND VEGETABLES

Macaroni Salad with Feta Cheese

Vegetables Piquant

Honeyed Sweet Potatoes

BREADS AND DESSERT

Garlic and Parsley Loaf

Romance Cookies

Pat's Wedding Punch

Yield: 6 to 7 gallons

My friend Pat Robinson has consulted on, decorated, and attended more than one hundred weddings. She shared this punch recipe with me when I was planning my daughter's wedding. It serves a large crowd, is easy to freeze, and looks lovely in the punch bowl. You may want to divide this recipe in half if you do not have pots or containers large enough to hold all of the ingredients.

6	3-ounce packages cherry- or strawberry-flavored gelatin
15	cups sugar
6	cups boiling water
2	gallons plus 2½ quarts cold water
6	10- to 12-ounce cans frozen lemon juice concentrate
6	46-ounce cans unsweetened pineapple juice
3 to 6	teaspoons almond extract, to taste
	Sliced oranges, strawberries, lemons, and cherries, for garnish
6 to 7	2-liter bottles ginger ale, chilled

Dissolve the gelatin and sugar in the boiling water in a large container. Add the cold water, lemon juice, pineapple juice, and almond extract. Place the sliced fruit in the bottom of quart- or gallon-sized containers (plastic tubs with lids are best). Fill the containers with punch, cover, and freeze overnight or until the punch hardens. Remove the frozen punch from the freezer 2 or 3 hours before serving so that parts of it become slushy. Place a container of the punch in a bowl and fill the bowl with the ginger ale. No ice is needed.

QUICK TIP: *Decorate the punch table with swirls of ribbon in the same colors chosen for the wedding.*

Gala Salmon Roll

Yield: 10-inch log

 1 15½-ounce can red salmon
 1 8-ounce package cream cheese, softened
 1 tablespoon freshly squeezed lemon juice
 2 teaspoons grated yellow onion
 1 teaspoon prepared horseradish
 ¼ teaspoon bottled liquid smoke seasoning or Worcestershire sauce
 ½ cup chopped pecans
 3 tablespoons minced fresh parsley, plus sprigs of fresh parsley
    for garnish
    Crackers

Drain the salmon and flake the meat with a fork. Combine the salmon, cream cheese, lemon juice, onion, horseradish, and liquid smoke in a large bowl and stir well. Chill several hours or overnight.

Place the salmon mixture on a serving platter and shape it into a log. Combine the pecans and parsley in a small bowl. Roll the log in the pecan mixture, pressing excess into the sides. Chill several hours. Serve on a platter surrounded by the sprigs of parsley and crackers.

QUICK TIP: *Small brooms tied with kente cloth ribbon and decorated with artificial flowers make pretty, ethnically inspired table decorations. Some brooms are prescented; if yours aren't and you would like them to be, insert a few sticks of cinnamon in with the flowers.*

Festive Fruit Salad

Yield: 8 to 10 Servings

"Talking with one another is loving one another." — Kenyan proverb

> 4 bananas, peeled and sliced
> 4 medium apples, unpeeled, seeded, and diced
> 2 cantaloupes, seeded, flesh scooped into balls
> 2 honeydew melons, seeded, flesh scooped into balls
> 2 cups sliced strawberries
> 2 cups blueberries
> 4 medium peaches, pitted and sliced
> ¼ cup freshly squeezed lemon juice
> 6 tablespoons confectioners' sugar, or to taste
>   Fresh mint sprigs, for garnish

Combine the bananas, apples, cantaloupes, melon balls, strawberries, blueberries, peaches, and lemon juice in a large bowl (the lemon juice retains the fruit's color and keeps it from turning brown). Place the fruit on individual serving dishes and, using a strainer or sifter, dust with the confectioners' sugar. Place a sprig of mint on top of each serving.

Marinated Chicken with Bananas

Yield: 8 Servings

"Love stretches your heart and makes you big inside." — Margaret Walker, poet, author of *Jubilee*

  2 2 1/2-pound broiler-fryers, washed and cut into serving pieces
1/3 cup freshly squeezed lemon juice
1/3 cup vegetable oil
  1 clove garlic, crushed
1 1/2 teaspoons dried thyme leaves
1 1/2 teaspoons salt
1/8 teaspoon freshly ground black pepper
1/8 teaspoon ground nutmeg
  8 medium bananas
  3 tablespoons dark corn syrup
    Lemon quarters, for garnish

Arrange the chicken pieces in a single layer in 2 large shallow baking pans. Combine the lemon juice, oil, garlic, thyme, salt, pepper, and nutmeg in a medium bowl and mix well. Pour the marinade over the chicken, cover, and refrigerate for several hours or overnight, turning the chicken several times.

When ready to cook the chicken, preheat the broiler and pour off the marinade but reserve it for basting. Broil the chicken, skin side down, in the same pan, about 8 inches from heat source, for about 25 minutes, basting with the reserved marinade. Turn the pieces over and broil for another 20 minutes, basting several times. Peel the bananas, arrange in the pan with the chicken, and brush with the corn syrup. Broil the chicken and bananas another 10 minutes or until the bananas are golden brown. Garnish with lemon quarters.

Macaroni Salad with Feta Cheese

Yield: 6 Servings

"Ah! this love. Tis a queer thing, but very amusing—to lookers-ons."
— Charlotte L. Forten Grimke, teacher and abolitionist

Salad Dressing
1/4 cup vegetable oil
2 tablespoons freshly squeezed lemon juice
2 tablespoons red wine vinegar
1 teaspoon dried oregano leaves
1/2 teaspoon salt
1/8 teaspoon freshly ground black pepper

Salad
1 8-ounce package elbow macaroni or bowtie pasta
1 cup 1/8-inch-wide green bell pepper strips
1 large tomato, halved lengthwise and thinly sliced
1/2 cup sliced green onion
8 ounces feta cheese, cubed
1/2 cup pitted black olives
2 tablespoons snipped fresh dill *or* 1 teaspoon dried dillweed

Combine the oil, lemon juice, vinegar, oregano, salt, and pepper in a container with a tight-fitting lid and shake until the ingredients are well blended. Cook the pasta according to the package directions. Drain. Combine the pasta and salad dressing in a large bowl, tossing well until the pasta is well coated. Cool. Stir in the green pepper, tomato, green onion, feta cheese, black olives, and dill. Cover and refrigerate. Chill 1 hour, mixing the salad again before serving.

Vegetables Piquant

Yield: 8 Servings

"Love has no fear."—Gikuyu proverb

    8 ounces baby carrots
    4 ounces whole pearl onions, peeled
    1 14-ounce can artichoke hearts, halved
    1 9-ounce package frozen whole green beans, thawed
    1 2-ounce jar sliced pimientos
    1 cup large, pitted ripe olives, black or green

Marinade:
    1 cup olive or vegetable oil
  $^1/_3$ cup red wine vinegar
    3 small cloves garlic, crushed
    1 teaspoon dried basil leaves
  $^3/_4$ teaspoon crushed red pepper
  $^1/_2$ teaspoon salt
    6 black peppercorns

Cover the carrots and onions with water and cook in a medium saucepan until tender-crisp, 10 to 12 minutes. Drain. Combine the carrots and onions with the artichoke hearts, green beans, pimientos, and olives in a 5-cup container with a tight-fitting lid. Combine the oil, vinegar, garlic, basil, red pepper, salt, and peppercorns in a small saucepan and bring to a boil. Pour the marinade over the vegetables. Cool, cover, and chill.

Honeyed Sweet Potatoes

Yield: 8 Servings

"The yams always taste sweet on the honeymoon."—African proverb

    4 **medium-sized sweet potatoes**
    2 **tablespoons butter or margarine, softened**
  $1/4$ **cup honey**
  $1/4$ **teaspoon salt**
  $1/4$ **teaspoon ground cinnamon**
  $1/2$ **teaspoon nutmeg**

Preheat the oven to 350 degrees. Arrange the sweet potatoes on a baking sheet or in a baking pan and bake until fork-tender, 1 to $1^1/2$ hours. (Alternatively, place the sweet potatoes in a spoke wheel arrangement with the smallest ends in the middle and microwave on high for 15 to 18 minutes or until fork-tender.)

When the sweet potatoes are cool enough to handle, slice each one lengthwise and set aside. Combine the softened butter, honey, and salt in a small bowl, then spread over each potato half. Score the flesh of the potato with a fork to fluff. Sprinkle with the nutmeg and cinnamon and place on a baking sheet. Return the potatoes to the oven to warm and combine flavors, about 4 minutes, or microwave for 1 minute.

Garlic and Parsley Loaf

Yield: 2 loaves

If you can find the large bulbs of garlic known as elephant garlic, use them for this recipe. Elephant garlic has a mild, sweet yet garlicky flavor and a creamy texture when baked. If you can't find elephant garlic, its smaller cousin will do.

16 cloves garlic
 2 large unsliced loaves French bread
¹/₄ cup butter or margarine, softened
 4 teaspoons dried parsley flakes

Preheat the oven to 400 degrees. Separate the cloves of garlic, brushing off any debris that may cling to them. Do not wash or remove the peel. Place the garlic on a small ungreased baking sheet and bake for 30 minutes. Remove the garlic from the oven and cool slightly. The outside of the garlic will be crisp and the inside will be creamy.

Cut each loaf of bread in half lengthwise and spread the butter on each half. Squeeze the garlic to crack open the skin and spread the creamy insides over the bread halves. Sprinkle with the parsley. Place the bread under the broiler for 30 seconds to warm.

Romance Cookies

Yield: 20 to 24 Cookies

I don't know how these Caribbean coconut cookies got their name, but I'll bet it's a sweet story.

>   1 cup butter or margarine
>   1/2 cup granulated sugar
>   2 cups plus 2 tablespoons all-purpose flour
>   1 teaspoon salt
>   2 eggs
> 11/2 cups firmly packed brown sugar
>   3/4 teaspoon baking powder
>   1 teaspoon vanilla
>   1 cup sweetened shredded coconut
>   Powdered sugar, for dusting
>   Ice cream, for serving

Preheat the oven to 350 degrees. Blend the butter and granulated sugar in a medium bowl until creamy. Sift 2 cups of the flour and the salt into a separate bowl, then add to the butter/sugar mixture and mix until well blended. Spread evenly into a 15 × 9-inch pan and bake for 10 minutes or until brown. Remove from the oven and set aside to cool.

Beat the eggs until foamy in a medium bowl. Add the brown sugar, the remaining 2 tablespoons flour, the baking powder, and vanilla. Mix well. Fold in the coconut. Spread this mixture on top of baked cookie layer, then return to the oven and bake another 20 minutes or until the top is golden brown and firm. Let cool and then cut into bars. Dust the bars with powdered sugar and store in an airtight container. Serve with scoops of ice cream.

July

Fourth of July Family Reunion Barbecue

There's nothing like getting together with your family. If a gathering of the clan is long overdue, it's time to plan a family reunion. As with any event, organization is the key. Forming a committee and assigning different tasks to each committee member is one of the easiest ways to bring everyone together for the big day. If you have several family members who live in your town and can come to a formal meeting, call them together. You can also plan meetings and exchange information via e-mail, faxes, letters, and phone calls.

Many family reunions are held from June through September, and often African-Americans plan their reunions on the fourth of July. You may want to start planning your reunion during other traditional holidays such as Thanksgiving, Christmas, or Kwanzaa, which will give out-of-towners enough time to schedule their summer vacations accordingly. You can also include "feelers" or information about the family reunion with your Christmas or Kwanzaa cards. This saves time and postage and will let you know how many people are interested in assisting with the planning and attending. Early notices are also a good way to start the fund-raising process if the expense of the event will be shared by the group. Collecting the money in advance will give you an accurate gauge of how large (or small) your budget will be.

Keep an accurate record of your finances, all the people you've contacted, and the progress you've made on everything from choosing the site to planning the entertainment. Not only will it make your job easier, it will help when it's time to organize the next reunion. Don't discard outdated addresses and phone numbers, as this information could prove useful if you lose track of certain relatives. In addition, the Red Cross may be able to assist you in finding long lost family members, and phone books for every city in the United States can usually be found at the library. (The library will also have books devoted to planning family reunions, as well as tracing missing persons.) You might also place notices in African-American community newspapers in the areas where most of your family members are concentrated. The ads are not very expensive and they are a good way to announce the reunion to people you may have been unable to contact.

Planning your family reunion in a city with activities of special interest to African-Americans is fun, educational, and entertaining. If your family lives near Atlanta, consider touring the home of Dr. Martin Luther King and the King Center. Or you may want to visit Colonial Williamsburg, between Norfolk and Richmond, Virginia, and go on the "Other Half Tour," which explores the lives of African-Americans during the eighteenth century. If a lot of family members will be visiting the city where the reunion will be held for the first time, consider arranging tours of the city and visits to African-American museums and art galleries, or offer to obtain group tickets to performances and other special events.

If your family is anything like mine, food will play a large role in the occasion. It's simplest to collect the money for food and prepare it all at once with the help of a cooking committee. I've found that this system works better than waiting on "Aunt Onetta" to arrive with the chicken, or "Cousin Fanika" to bring twenty bags of ice so you can start serving the drinks. To give people who are not on the cooking committee a chance to contribute, ask everyone to bring a dessert.

FOURTH OF JULY FAMILY REUNION BARBECUE MENU

SAUCES AND CONDIMENTS

Tangy Barbecue Sauce

Sweet Barbecue Sauce

Hot Barbecue Sauce

Texas Barbecue Sauce

DRINKS

Mint Tea

MAIN DISHES

Barbecued Beef Brisket

Bourbon-glazed Baby Back Ribs

Barbecued Sausage

Grilled Chicken with Pepper Salsa

SIDE DISHES

Easy Ranch-Style Pinto Beans

Reunion Coleslaw

Lone Star Potato Salad

Tangy Barbecue Sauce

Yield: 4¹/₂ cups

¹/₂ cup vegetable shortening
  1 small lemon, thinly sliced
¹/₂ medium-sized yellow onion, finely chopped
  1 clove garlic, minced
  1 teaspoon chili powder
¹/₄ teaspoon ground black pepper
  2 cups distilled white vinegar
¹/₂ cup red wine vinegar

Melt the shortening over low heat in a large, nonaluminum saucepan. Add the lemon, onion, garlic, chili powder, pepper, and the vinegars, mixing well. Raise the heat to high and bring the mixture to a boil. Reduce the heat to medium and cook for 5 minutes, stirring occasionally.

QUICK TIP: *Send a scrap of fabric along with the invitation to the family reunion. Have each family member use a permanent marker to write his or her name, date of birth, and saying or drawing on the piece of fabric. Sew the scraps together to make an heirloom quilt. You can display it throughout the reunion and sell raffle tickets to family members who want to purchase it. The money from the raffle can go toward a scholarship fund for the children in the family or to a member of the family who is going through tough times.*

Sweet Barbecue Sauce

Yield: 4¹/₂ cups

Tomato-based sauces add a wonderful flavor to barbecued meats but tend to burn easily. To alleviate this problem, wait until the last few minutes of cooking before brushing the sauce on the meat.

3   cups canned tomato sauce or ketchup
1   medium-sized yellow onion, diced
2   stalks celery, sliced
    Juice of 1 lemon
2   cups water
2   tablespoons distilled white vinegar
2   tablespoons brown sugar, or more to taste
2   tablespoons molasses
2   tablespoons vegetable oil
¹/₂ teaspoon cayenne pepper

Combine the tomato sauce, onion, celery, lemon juice, water, vinegar, brown sugar, molasses, vegetable oil, and cayenne pepper in a large, nonaluminum pan, over medium heat. Bring the mixture to a low simmer and cook for 20 minutes, stirring occasionally.

Hot Barbecue Sauce

Yield: 4 1/2 cups

For a hotter sauce, add 1 tablespoon Worcestershire sauce and 1 tea-spoon Tabasco sauce or hot salsa. Wait 5 or 10 minutes to taste, then add more as desired. Always allow the sauce to simmer a while before adding any more "heat" to it.

3 cups tomato sauce or ketchup
2 cups water
1 green bell pepper, diced
1 medium-sized yellow onion, diced
2 stalks celery, diced
1 clove garlic, peeled and diced
2 tablespoons vegetable oil
2 tablespoons distilled white vinegar
   Juice of 1 lemon
2 teaspoons cayenne pepper
1 teaspoon soy sauce
1 teaspoon chili powder
1 teaspoon Tabasco sauce
1 bay leaf

Combine the tomato sauce, water, green pepper, onion, celery, garlic, vegetable oil, vinegar, lemon juice, cayenne pepper, soy sauce, chili powder, Tabasco sauce, and bay leaf in a large, non-aluminum pan over medium-low heat and cook for 20 minutes, stirring occasionally. Reduce the heat to a low simmer and cook for another 20 minutes, stirring occasionally.

QUICK TIP: *Use family photos as decorations for the table or display them collage-style on a large sheet of cardboard. Putting the board in a central area creates a wonderful conversation piece that is sure to invoke pleasant memories.*

Texas Barbecue Sauce

Yield: 4¹/₂ cups

   3 cups ketchup
   2 cups water
   1 cup finely chopped yellow onion
   2 tablespoons finely chopped garlic
   2 or more jalapeño peppers, seeded and finely chopped
   3 tablespoons Worcestershire sauce
   2 tablespoons soy sauce
   1 tablespoon extra-virgin olive oil
   1 tablespoon cider vinegar
   1 tablespoon firmly packed brown sugar
   2 teaspoons ground ginger
1¹/₂ teaspoons dry mustard

Combine the ketchup, water, onion, garlic, jalapeños, Worcestershire sauce, soy sauce, olive oil, vinegar, brown sugar, ginger, and dry mustard in a large, nonaluminum pan over low heat and cook for 50 minutes, stirring occasionally. If the sauce is too thick, add a little more water. This sauce can be stored in an airtight container for 1 to 2 weeks.

QUICK TIP: *A family reunion provides the perfect opportunity to fill in the family tree, especially if you have older members of the family in attendance who can remember the names of some of your ancestors. Assign a committee member to gather the information and fill in the blanks.*

Mint Tea

Yield: 5 gallons

- 16 Orange Pekoe tea bags
- 6 cups sugar
  Approximately 50 mint leaves
  Zest of 6 lemons
  Juice of 18 lemons
- 6 cups pineapple juice
- 4 gallons cold water

Place the tea bags in a large pot and cover with 3 quarts boiling water. Cover the pot and allow the tea to steep for 8 minutes. Combine 2 quarts water and the sugar in a medium pot over low heat and cook, stirring continuously, until a syrup forms. Stir in the mint leaves and the lemon zest. Remove the pot from the heat, cover and set aside for 10 minutes. When ready, stir the sugar mixture into the tea, cover, and steep for 10 minutes. Strain the mixture into a large container. Add the lemon juice, pineapple juice, and 4 gallons of cold water. Mix well and serve over ice.

Barbecued Beef Brisket

Yield: 12 Servings

Mesquite coals
1 4-to 6-pound beef brisket slab
2 tablespoons extra-virgin olive oil
1½ teaspoons freshly ground black pepper
1½ teaspoons freshly ground white pepper
¾ teaspoon paprika
½ teaspoon ground cumin
1 tablespoon salt
Mesquite chips (optional)

Using mesquite charcoal, build a good-sized fire in a large grill. When the coals are medium-hot and covered with a grayish ash, divide them in half with a pair of long tongs. Push half of the hot coals to one end of the grill and half to the opposite end. Make a drip pan out of aluminum foil if the grill is not equipped with one and center the drip pan on the bottom of the grill. Season the brisket with the olive oil, black pepper, white pepper, paprika, cumin, and salt. Rub the seasoning into the meat. Allow the brisket to marinate at room temperature for 30 minutes. Place the brisket in the center of the grill rack and cover. Partly close the dampers to control the burning. Cook the meat for 4 hours, turning it and checking the coals every hour. If the fire is too cool, open the dampers slightly. If the fat in the drip pan is sizzling, the fire may be too hot; close the dampers slightly. The objective is to achieve a steady, even heat throughout the cooking process. After 4 hours, if the fire is still burning well, you may want to place a handful of wet mesquite chips over the coals.

Turn the brisket, brush with the sauce of your choice (see pages 185–189), cover, and cook for another 30 minutes. Remove the brisket from the grill. Let stand for 10 minutes before slicing. Slice meat against the grain.

Bourbon-glazed Baby Back Ribs

Yield: 12 Servings

10 pounds baby back ribs
 1 cup bourbon
$^1/_2$ cup honey
$^1/_4$ cup peanut oil
$^1/_4$ cup soy sauce
 3 cloves garlic, mashed and diced
    Mesquite charcoal
    Salt and freshly ground black pepper

Place the racks of ribs in 2 or 3 shallow glass pans. Combine the bourbon, honey, oil, soy sauce, and garlic in a medium bowl. Brush the ribs with the marinade, coating all sides well. Let the ribs stand at room temperature for 30 minutes.

Using mesquite charcoal, build a good-sized fire in a large grill. When the coals are medium-hot and covered with a grayish ash, divide them in half with a pair of long tongs. Push half of the hot coals to one end of the grill and half to the opposite end. Make a drip pan out of aluminum foil if the grill is not equiped with one and center it in the bottom of the grill.

Sprinkle the ribs with the salt and pepper. Place the ribs in the center of the grill rack and cover. Partly close the dampers to control the burning. Cook the meat for 15 minutes. Turn the meat and baste it again. Cook for another 15 minutes, then turn and baste again. Cook 5 to 10 minutes longer or until the ribs are crispy and the juices run yellow when the thickest part of the meat is pricked with a fork.

Remove the ribs from the grill. Let the ribs rest for 10 minutes before carving.

QUICK TIP: *Plan a talent show for your family reunion. It will be entertaining and will also give everyone a chance to see if any of the talent in the family is hereditary.*

Barbecued Sausage

Yield: 12 Servings

Mesquite charcoal
2 pounds smoked sausage, uncooked
1½ cups homemade (see pages 185–189) or store-bought
barbecue sauce

Using mesquite charcoal, build a good-sized fire in a large grill. When the coals are medium-hot and covered with a grayish ash, place the sausage on the grill. Grill the sausage for 15 minutes, then turn with tongs and baste with barbecue sauce. Continue cooking the sausage for 1 hour 15 minutes, turning and basting every 15 minutes. To serve, cut the sausage into 1-inch slices.

QUICK TIP: *Holding a memorial service for those who are deceased is a way to bond the family together. For the opening of the reunion, arrange for a short service with a minister or plan a "calling of the names" ceremony, acknowledging the absence of deceased family members. A moment of silence serves as a nice tribute.*

Grilled Chicken with Pepper Salsa

Yield: 12 Servings

Bell Pepper Salsa:

- 4 large red or yellow tomatoes, seeded and chopped
- 1/2 cup finely chopped purple onion
- 1/2 cup red bell pepper, chopped
- 1/2 cup green bell pepper, chopped
- 1/4 cup finely chopped cilantro
- 2 large cloves garlic, minced
- 2 tablespoons freshly squeezed lime juice
- 1 tablespoon seeded and minced jalapeño pepper
- 1 teaspoon sugar
- 1 teaspoon salt
- 1/2 teaspoon ground cumin

Chicken:

- 12 chicken breast halves
- 1/2 cup freshly squeezed lime juice
- 1/2 cup virgin olive oil
- 1 teaspoon chili powder
- 1 teaspoon ground black pepper
- Mesquite charcoal
- Avocado slices and cilantro sprigs, for garnish

To make the salsa, combine the tomatoes, onion, red and green pepper, cilantro, garlic, lime juice, jalapeño pepper, sugar, salt, and cumin in a medium bowl and mix until well blended. Let the salsa sit for an hour at room temperature before serving.

To make the chicken, place the breasts in 2 large glass baking dishes. Combine the lime juice, oil, chili powder, and pepper in a small bowl and mix well. Pour the mixture over the chicken, dividing the marinade evenly between the pans. Turn the chicken to coat, then cover and refrigerate for at least an hour. Using mesquite charcoal, build a good-sized fire in a large grill. When the coals are medium-hot and covered with a grayish ash, place the chicken on the grill, skin side down, at least 8 inches from the heat. Cover and grill for 8 to 10 minutes. Turn the chicken and grill for another 8 to 10 minutes or until a fork can be inserted in the chicken easily and the juices run clear, not pink. Place the chicken on a serving platter, garnish with avocado slices and sprigs of cilantro, and serve with the salsa.

QUICK TIP: *You may want to have a family swap meet and sale during your family reunion. This will give family members an opportunity to swap or buy handmade items from each other.*

Easy Ranch-Style Pinto Beans

Yield: 12 Servings

5 23-ounce cans red pinto beans, drained
1 cup barbecue sauce, homemade (see pages 185–189)
   or store bought
1 cup mild salsa
3/4 cup firmly packed brown sugar

Combine the beans, barbecue sauce, salsa, and brown sugar in a large pot and simmer over low heat until warm, about 10 minutes, stirring occasionally to keep the beans from sticking.

QUICK TIP: *When organizing your committees, don't forget about a clean-up crew. Otherwise, a few people may find themselves doing all the work.*

Reunion Coleslaw

Yield: 12 Servings

2 heads cabbage, shredded (about 20 cups)
4 medium Spanish onions, cut into rings
2 large green bell peppers, cut into rings
2 cups plus 4 teaspoons sugar
2 cups distilled white vinegar
1½ cups vegetable oil
2 tablespoons salt
2 teaspoons dry mustard
2 teaspoons celery seed

Layer the cabbage, onion, and green pepper in a large bowl. Sprinkle 2 cups of the sugar across the top.

Combine the remaining 4 teaspoons sugar, the vinegar, salad oil, salt, dry mustard, and celery seed in a medium saucepan over medium heat and mix well. Raise the heat to high and bring the mixture to a boil, stirring constantly. Pour over the slaw, cover, and refrigerate for at least 4 hours. Before serving, toss the salad well.

QUICK TIP: *Colored T-shirts are a great way to sort out family members. They can help everyone identify branches of the family tree as well as find folks (especially children) in a crowd. Choose a group of colors and use them as a color code from the initial planning stages to the final event. If desired, have the T-shirts screenprinted with the name and date of the reunion.*

Lone Star Potato Salad

Yield: 12 Servings

12 medium potatoes, boiled with their skins on, cooled, peeled, and diced
 6 hard-cooked eggs, diced, and 2 hard-cooked eggs, sliced
 1 cup low-fat mayonnaise
 4 tablespoons mustard
 1 cup diced celery
²/₃ cup grated yellow onion
¹/₂ large green bell pepper, seeded and minced
¹/₄ cup sweet pickle relish
¹/₄ cup dill pickle relish
 2 tablespoons sugar
 1 teaspoon celery salt
 1 teaspoon garlic salt
    Paprika and pimiento, for garnish (optional)

Combine the potatoes, diced eggs, salad dressing, and mustard in a large bowl and mix well. Add the celery, onion, bell pepper, sweet and dill pickle relishes, sugar, celery salt, and garlic salt and mix well. Cover and chill. Before serving, garnish with the sliced hard-cooked eggs, paprika, and pimiento.

August

Young Adult Rites of Passage Dinner

Many African-American parents as well as many organizations, from churches to social groups, have begun to embrace the ancient African tradition of the rites of passage ceremony as a way of recognizing their children's budding maturity while grounding them in the traditions of our culture.

African rites of passage or coming of age ceremonies vary from region to region. In Ghana, as in many other African regions, the ceremonies center around fertility and recognizing a child's passage from youth to adulthood. The girls and boys go through a period of preparation which ends with an elaborate celebration.

Three good sources of information about planning a ceremony are *Transformation: A Rites of Passage Manual for African-American Girls*, *Bringing the Black Boy to Manhood: The Passage*, and *The African Centered Rite of Passage and Education*. The personnel at your local library or bookstore may be able to recommend other books.

The rites of passage ceremony is a long process. Generally it takes about nine months, during which time initiates study African rites of passage, their family history, and the history of our people. They are also taught about sex education, spirituality and community spirit, personal hygiene, housekeeping and finances, assertiveness and leadership, values, planning for the future, time management, organizational skills, and African techniques of art and dance. The classes are taught by parents or community leaders.

During the final part of the initiation rites, the initiates live together while preparing and rehearsing for the rites of passage ceremony and celebration. If you start the process in December, the final stages of the initiation are held over the summer, giving the initiates something worthwhile to do with their free time and an opportunity to bond together. I like the symbolism of starting the rites of passage process during Kwanzaa and ending with the ceremony in August, nine months later, a celebration of the rebirth of the children into young adults.

The final ceremony begins with a thirty- to forty-five-minute period of entertainment featuring everything from poetry readings to musical selections. The initiates dress in African-style clothing and come into the room in a procession. The leader of the ceremony explains the initiation process, presents each child to the community, and asks for their blessing. The audience responds by saying Yebo! Yebo! Yebo! which is a Zulu word for "yes." The ceremony leader, the parents, and each initiate give a speech. Then the ceremony leader says a prayer, and the passage ritual begins. At ceremonies for young girls, the mothers usually wrap the girls' heads with a gele, a long piece of fabric that is worn as a headdress, and they are given a bracelet, necklace, or other piece of jewelry. Boys can be given an African walking stick or fly whisk (which was used by African royalty). Although the initiation periods for boys and girls are done separately, the rites of passage ceremonies can be held together.

After closing remarks by the ceremony leader, the initiates perform the African dances they've learned during the initiation process. The audience joins in for a final group song and the ceremony comes to a close as the young adults pass through the audience to form a reception line.

In keeping with African tradition, after the ceremony, food is served. The menu I have designed reflects our African culture and embraces our contributions to American culinary cuisine.

YOUNG ADULT RITES OF PASSAGE DINNER

DRINKS AND APPETIZERS

African Fruit Punch

Ghana Plantain Appetizer

North African Orange Salad

MAIN DISHES

Lemon Chicken with Onions

Creole Rice Cakes with Spicy Tomato and Shrimp Sauce

VEGETABLES

Ethiopian-Style Vegetables

DESSERT

Sweet Potato Pound Cake

Tanzanian Baked Bananas

African Fruit Punch

Yield: 6½ cups

2½ cups lemonade
1 cup orange juice
1 cup pineapple juice
1 cup papaya juice or peach necter

Combine the lemonade and orange, pineapple, and papaya juices and chill. Serve over ice.

QUICK TIP: *Decorate the place where the rites of passage ceremony is held with African art work, fabrics, and baskets of fruits and vegetables. African fertility dolls are an important part of traditional African ceremonies. You may want to display some of them as centerpieces on the serving table.*

Ghana Plantain Appetizer

Yield: 6 Servings

This appetizer, known as kelewele *in Ghana, tastes similar to American potato chips and is sure to be a hit with teenagers.*

> 3 cups cooking oil
> 2 tablespoons water
> 1 teaspoon ground ginger
> 1/2 teaspoon salt
> 1/2 teaspoon cayenne pepper
> 6 large unripened plantains, peeled and sliced 1/2 inch thick

Heat the oil until it is hot but not smoking in a deep-fryer or a skillet deep enough to cover the plantain slices. Combine the water, ginger, salt, and cayenne pepper in a small bowl. One by one, drop the plantain slices into the bowl, coating each piece evenly. Deep-fry the plantain slices until golden brown. Drain on paper towels.

North African Orange Salad

Yield: 8 Servings

I love the texture and taste of this salad. It makes a wonderful summertime appetizer.

  1 **large head iceberg lettuce, shredded**
  1 **large onion, thinly sliced**
 16 **Greek olives, pitted and chopped**
  2 **large oranges, peeled and thinly sliced**

Dressing:
  1 **cup virgin olive oil**
 $^1/_2$ **cup freshly squeezed lemon juice, strained**
  1 **teaspoon salt**
 $^1/_4$ **teaspoon cayenne pepper**

Toss the lettuce, onion, and olives in a salad bowl. Arrange the orange slices on top.

To make the dressing, whisk together the oil, lemon juice, salt, and pepper and drizzle over the salad. Cover and refrigerate until ready to serve.

Lemon Chicken with Onions

Yield: 8 Servings

This savory African dish is best when the chicken is allowed to marinate in the lemon juice and spices for at least 24 hours. It can also be cooked a day in advance, then reheated. I pull out this recipe when I am expecting lots of company and do not have a lot of time to prepare.

        4 cups sliced onions
        6 cloves garlic, peeled and minced
        1 teaspoon minced fresh hot green chiles
        1 tablespoon salt
        2 teaspoons white pepper
        1 teaspoon ground ginger
        1 cup freshly squeezed lemon juice
     2$^{1}/_{2}$ cups water
       $^{1}/_{2}$ cup plus 2 tablespoons peanut oil
        2 (2- to 3-pound) chickens, quartered

Combine the onions, garlic, chiles, salt, white pepper, and ginger in a large baking dish. Stir in the lemon juice, 1 cup of the water, and 2 tablespoons of the oil. Add the chicken pieces, turn to coat with the marinade, then refrigerate for at least 4 hours, turning the pieces every 30 minutes.

Remove the chicken from the marinade, reserving the marinade, and pat the pieces dry with paper towels. Heat the remaining $^{1}/_{2}$ cup of oil in a skillet until hot but not smoking. Add the chicken to the hot oil a few pieces at a time and cook, turning frequently, for 3 to 5 minutes to brown evenly. Pour off all but about 2 tablespoons oil from the skillet and remove the skillet from the heat.

Using the back of a spoon, press the marinade through a fine sieve set over a bowl, retaining both the solids in the sieve and the liquid in the bowl. Reheat the oil in the skillet and add the solids from the sieve. Cook, stirring constantly, until the onions are transparent, about 3 minutes.

Return the chicken to the skillet and add ½ cup of the strained marinade liquid and the remaining ½ cup water. Bring to a boil over high heat. Partially cover the pan, reduce the heat, and simmer for about 25 minutes or until the chicken is tender.

Creole Rice Cakes with Spicy Tomato and Shrimp Sauce

Yield: 12 Servings

A Creole dish is traditionally spicy and contains tomatoes, onions, and peppers. Many Creole dishes are a mixture of varied African cooking techniques and spices. This delicious dish appears to be complicated but is really fairly simple to prepare and well worth the effort. The rice cakes remind me of traditional African foofoo in texture. Foofoo (also known as fufu, foufou, pap and putu) is the starchy accompaniment to many main dishes in Africa. For years African women have pounded dried yams, cassava slices, corn kernels, plantain, or rice into flour to make foofoo. It has the consistency of a dumpling and is usually shaped into a ball. If you are expecting vegetarian guests or know of guests who do not eat shellfish, cook the shrimp separately (not in the tomato sauce) and serve it in a separate bowl.

Spicy Tomato Sauce:
- 1/4 cup vegetable oil
- 2 cups chopped yellow onion
- 1 1/2 cups chopped green bell pepper
- 1 1/2 cups diced celery
- 4 8-ounce cans tomato sauce
- 2 cups chicken broth
- 1 tablespoon salsa
- 1 tablespoon dried oregano leaves
- 1 teaspoon ground cumin
- 1 1/2 pounds shelled, tiny shrimp, cooked

Rice Cakes:

4 eggs
3 cups long-grain white rice, cooked and cooled
1 cup oat bran
   Lemon or lime wedges (for garnish)

To make the tomato sauce, heat the oil in a medium pan over low heat. Add the onion, bell pepper, and celery and sauté until tender, about 10 minutes. Stir in the tomato sauce, broth, salsa, oregano, and cumin and bring to a boil. Reduce the heat to a simmer and cook, uncovered, for 10 minutes. Remove from the heat. Set aside 1 cup of the sauce to add to the rice cake mixture.

To make the rice cakes, preheat the oven to 350 degrees. Beat the eggs in a large bowl until foamy. Add the rice, oat bran, and one cup of the tomato sauce. Mix well.

Grease one 12-cup or two 6-cup muffin tins. Divide the rice mixture evenly among the cups. Bake until the rice cakes are dry to the touch, about 25 minutes. Cool the cakes slightly. Slide a knife around the edge of each cake to remove it from the tin and place the cakes on individual serving plates.

Reheat the tomato sauce. Add the shrimp, cooking for 1 minute to heat. Ladle the sauce over the cakes. Garnish each plate with a lemon or lime wedge.

Ethiopian-Style Vegetables

Yield: 8 Servings

This dish is traditionally served as a main course during Lent in Ethiopia, where it is known as yataklete kilkil. *It is also a tasty side dish.*

1¼ teaspoons salt

6 small potatoes

3 carrots, scraped and sliced

6 green onions (including tops), chopped

1½ cups fresh green beans, washed, ends removed, and cut crosswise into 1-inch pieces

or 1 9-ounce package frozen cut green beans

2 medium onions, thinly sliced

1 green bell pepper, seeded and cut into strips

½ teaspoon chopped jalapeño pepper, ribs and seeds removed

1 clove garlic, chopped

1 teaspoon powdered ginger

½ teaspoon white pepper

3 tablespoons olive oil

Bring 4 cups water to boil in a medium pot, then add ¼ teaspoon of the salt. Peel the potatoes and slice them into rounds, placing the rounds in a bowl of cold water as you work to prevent discoloration. Drop the potato slices into the boiling water. (The water should cover the potatoes completely.) Add the carrots, green onions, and green beans. Bring the vegetables to a rolling boil and cook for 5 minutes.

Do not cover the pan. Drain the vegetables in a large colander, then rinse with cold water. Set aside in the colander to drain completely.

Heat the oil in a heavy saucepan. Add the onions, bell pepper, and jalapeño, and sauté over low heat until the vegetables are soft but not brown, about 5 minutes. Stir in the garlic, ginger, the remaining teaspoon salt, and the white pepper. Add the potatoes, carrots, green onion, and green beans, and stir until the vegetables are coated with the oil mixture. Partially cover the pan and continue cooking for about 10 minutes or until the vegetables are tender but still somewhat crisp.

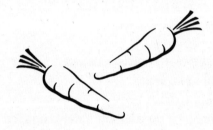

Sweet Potato Pound Cake

Yield: 10-inch cake

1/2 cup vegetable shortening
1/2 cup butter or margarine, softened
 2 cups sugar
 6 eggs
 3 cups all-purpose flour
 1 teaspoon baking powder
1/2 teaspoon salt
1/4 teaspoon baking soda
 1 cup buttermilk
1 1/2 cups canned cut sweet potatoes, drained, mashed, and strained
1/2 teaspoon almond extract
1/4 teaspoon coconut extract
1/4 cup slivered almonds, toasted and finely chopped
1/4 cup sweetened flaked coconut

Preheat the oven to 350 degrees. Grease and flour a 10-inch Bundt pan. Cream the shortening and butter in a large mixing bowl. Add the sugar, beating until the ingredients are fluffy and well blended. Add the eggs one at a time, beating well after each addition.

Sift the flour, baking powder, salt, and baking soda into a medium bowl. Alternately add a small amount of the flour mixture and the buttermilk to the sugar mixture, beginning and ending with the flour mixture. Stir in the sweet potatoes, almond extract, and coconut extract, mixing well.

Grease and flour a 10-inch Bundt pan. Sprinkle the almonds and coconut over the bottom of the pan. Pour the batter into the prepared

Bundt pan. Bake for 1 hour 15 minutes until a tester comes out clean. Cool on a wire rack for 10 minutes before removing the cake from the pan.

QUICK TIP: *During or after the ceremony you may want to display the reports that the initiates have done on their family history, African history and culture, and African rite of passage rituals.*

Tanzanian Baked Bananas

Yield: 8 Servings

4 large, ripe, *unpeeled* bananas
3 tablespoons brown sugar
2 tablespoons melted butter
1 teaspoon lemon juice

Preheat the oven to 425 degrees. Cut off the ends of the bananas. Place the unpeeled bananas on an ungreased cookie sheet or in a baking pan. Bake for 15 minutes or until the skins burst and turn black. Peel and discard the skins and cut the bananas lengthwise. Combine the brown sugar, butter, and lemon juice in a small bowl, then drizzle over the cooked bananas.

September

Honoring the Ancestors—
Parents' Day Dinner

It is an African tradition to treasure and respect the elderly. Our elders are our wealth. They are a living repository of history, the keepers of our customs and traditions, and the voice of experience.

I enjoy talking with older people. I love history, and to talk with someone who has actually lived through times I've only read about is inspiring.

Respect and admiration for one's elders must be taught. It is easy to look at a person who may be wrinkled and frail and overlook their value. Until you talk with a person, you can't fully appreciate them. As I grow older, I have more and more respect for my parents and grandparents and other people their age. My maternal grandparents are deceased, something that makes me treasure the elders that are left in my family even more. They've struggled, endured, and survived with an ageless grace and a wonderful sense of humor.

Treat your parents and grandparents to a dinner that's sure to make them feel special. Several of the recipes on this menu are old-fashioned favorites and may even bring back some memories.

HONORING THE ANCESTORS— PARENTS' DAY DINNER

DRINK

Mint Citrus Tea

MAIN DISH

Old-Fashioned Pot Roast with Potatoes and Carrots

SIDE DISHES

Creamed Spinach

Garlic Grits

BREADS AND DESSERTS

Double-Corn Muffins

Gingerbread with Lemon Sauce

Mint Citrus Tea

Yield: 2¹/₂ quarts

8 Orange Pekoe tea bags
6 fresh mint leaves
2 quarts boiling water
1 cup sugar
   Juice of 3 medium oranges (about 1 cup)
   Juice of 5 medium lemons (about 1 cup)

Place the tea bags and mint leaves in a large, heatproof container. Pour in the boiling water, cover, and let stand for about 7 minutes. Using a slotted spoon, remove the tea bags and mint leaves. Stir in the sugar, orange juice, and lemon juice. Serve over ice.

Old-Fashioned Pot Roast
with Potatoes and Carrots

Yield: 8 to 10 Servings

"It is the duty of children to wait on elders, and not the elders on children." — Kenyan proverb

    1 4-pound top or bottom round roast
    1 10³/₄-ounce can cream of mushroom soup
    1 cup dry red wine
    1 cup chopped yellow onion
    2 cloves garlic, minced
    1 tablespoon chopped fresh parsley
 1¹/₂ teaspoons salt
 1¹/₂ teaspoons freshly ground black pepper
    1 teaspoon allspice
   10 medium potatoes, scrubbed, peeled, and quartered
    6 carrots, scraped and cut into 2-inch pieces

Preheat the oven to 350 degrees. Place the roast in a large Dutch oven or roaster. Combine the mushroom soup and wine, mixing until well blended and smooth. Pour the wine mixture over the roast, turning the meat to coat it completely. Add the onion, garlic, parsley, salt, pepper, and allspice. Cover and bake for 1¹/₂ hours. Turn the heat down to 325 degrees. Baste the roast with the pan drippings. Lift the roast and place the potatoes and carrots on the bottom of the pan under the roast. Cover and continue baking for another 1¹/₂ hours until roast is brown and tender.

Creamed Spinach

Yield: 6 Servings

"The hand of a child can not reach the ledge; the hand of the elder can not enter the gourd; both the young and the old have what each can do for the other." — Yoruba proverb

        3 10-ounce packages frozen spinach
        4 tablespoons butter or margarine
        1 3-ounce package cream cheese
        2 tablespoons milk
        1 4-ounce can button mushrooms, sliced
        1 teaspoon mild salsa
        1 teaspoon salt
       2/3 cup bread crumbs

    Cook the spinach according to the package directions. Drain and set aside. Melt the butter in a medium saucepan over low heat. Add the cream cheese and milk and stir until the cream cheese softens and begins to melt, 3 to 5 minutes. Add the spinach, mushrooms, salsa, and salt, stirring until the ingredients are well blended and warm, 5 to 7 minutes. Place the spinach in a serving bowl and sprinkle with the bread crumbs.

Garlic Grits

Yield: 8 Servings

Grits are hip now but have always been a mainstay in our house-hold. This is a tasty twist on an old-fashioned breakfast favorite.

> 2 cups grits
> 1 pound sharp Cheddar cheese, grated
> 1/2 cup lowfat butter or margarine
> 3 tablespoons Worcestershire sauce
> 1 clove garlic, peeled and minced
> 1 1/2 teaspoons mild salsa
> 4 egg whites

Preheat the oven to 400 degrees. Grease a large, ovenproof casserole dish. Cook the grits according to the package directions. Place the cooked grits, cheese, butter, Worcestershire sauce, garlic, and salsa in the prepared casserole. Whip the egg whites in a medium bowl until soft peaks form. Gently fold the egg whites into the grits mixture. Bake for 20 minutes.

Double-Corn Muffins

Yield: 12 Muffins

"We often spend so much time bemoaning our loss of youth that we fail to appreciate the charm, the serenity, and the grace that can be ours as old women." — Dorothy R. Robinson, age 81, professional educator from Lavaca County, Texas

    1 cup sifted all-purpose flour
    1 cup yellow cornmeal
    ¼ cup sugar
    4 teaspoons baking powder
    1 teaspoon salt
    2 eggs, slightly beaten
    1 cup milk
    3 tablespoons butter or margarine, melted
    1 cup canned cream-style corn

Preheat the oven to 425 degrees. Lightly grease the bottoms only of 12 (3-inch) muffin pan cups. Sift the flour with the cornmeal, sugar, baking powder, and salt in a large bowl. Set aside.

Using a medium bowl and a wooden spoon, combine the eggs, milk, butter, and corn. Add the flour mixture, stirring until the moistened. Do not overmix; the batter will not be smooth. Spoon the batter into the muffin pan cups and bake for 20 to 25 minutes or until the tops are golden brown and a tester inserted in the center comes out clean.

Gingerbread with Lemon Sauce

Yield: 8 to 10 Servings

Don't skimp on ingredients for this dessert. The better the quality, the better your gingerbread will taste.

Gingerbread:
- 1 cup firmly packed brown sugar
- 1/2 cup vegetable shortening
- 2 eggs
- 3/4 cup molasses
- 2 3/4 cups all-purpose flour
- 2 teaspoons baking soda
- 2 teaspoons ground ginger
- 1 teaspoon ground cinnamon
- 1/2 teaspoon salt
- 1 cup buttermilk or sour milk (1 tablespoon of vinegar mixed with 1 cup milk)

Lemon Sauce:
- 1 cup sugar
- 1 egg, beaten
- 1 tablespoon butter
- juice of 1 lemon

To make the gingerbread, preheat the oven to 350 degrees. Grease and flour a 13 × 9 × 2-inch pan. Combine the sugar, shortening, and eggs in a large mixing bowl and mix well. Stir in the molasses. Sift the flour, soda, ginger, cinnamon, and salt in a medium bowl. Add small amounts of the flour mixture to the sugar mixture, alternating with the buttermilk until the ingredients are well blended. Spread the batter evenly into the prepared pan and bake for 35 to 40 minutes.

To make the lemon sauce, combine the sugar, egg, butter, and lemon juice in a small saucepan and cook over medium heat, stirring well, until thick, 8 to 10 minutes.

October

Heroes' Day Children's Party

African-American Heroes' Day was born of a desire to make Halloween more meaningful for African-American children, while, at the same time, retaining some of the elements of the holiday, such as dressing up in costumes and playing make-believe. For religious reasons, many people abhor the history behind Halloween, while others feel that trick-or-treating has become too dangerous.

The name of this celebration may differ from city to city, but the purpose is the same, to provide a safe, fun, positive, creative, and culturally enhancing holiday, especially for children.

A good way to prepare your children for African-American Heroes Day is to read to them or have them read biographies of famous African-Americans, then ask them to select one, and dress them up as him or her. If the party is going is be at your house, help your child make the invitations to the party, and be sure to invite the parents to stay, as you will need their help.

Plan a parade and ask each hero to tell the group a little about himself or herself. Give away extra prizes to the children who were able to recite something their hero actually said.

Keep the "treats" part of the holiday intact. This kid-pleasing menu should do the "trick."

HEROES' DAY CHILDREN'S PARTY MENU

DRINKS AND SALADS

Ali's Punch

Artistic Salad

MAIN DISH

Dr. Ben Carson's "Heart"-warming Chili

BREADS AND DESSERTS

Willie Mays' Home Run Bran Muffins

Angela's By-the-Book Brittle

Carver's Peanut Butter Cookies

Ali's Punch

Yield: 5 quarts

*A hollowed-out pumpkin makes a perfect "punch bowl" for this drink.
"To be a great champion you must believe you are the best. If
you're not, pretend you are."* — Muhammad Ali, boxer, businessman

$\frac{1}{2}$ gallon orange sherbet
1 46-ounce can pineapple juice, chilled
1 liter ginger ale, chilled
3 cups orange juice, chilled
3 cups lemon-lime soda, chilled

Scoop the sherbet into a large container. Add the pineapple juice,
ginger ale, orange juice, and lemon-lime soda, mixing well. (Chunks
of the orange sherbet will remain in the punch.) Serve chilled.

Artistic Salad

Yield: 8 Servings

This "hands-on" salad is fun for children to make and eat. Tell the children that they can munch on the ingredients while they work and eat the whole thing—except for the toothpicks—when they finish.

1	whole orange per person, peeled
16	carrot sticks
16	celery sticks
16	olives
16	zucchini slices
16	dill pickle slices
½	pound bean sprouts
16	cherry tomatoes
16	walnut halves
16	red and green bell pepper strips
16	cucumber slices
4	cups (1 head) shredded lettuce

Place the orange in the center of a paper plate and surround with a small amount of all of the other ingredients. Using toothpicks, attach ingredients to the orange.

QUICK TIP: *This is a good time to show children pictures of the work of some famous African-American collage artists, such as Romare Bearden.*

Dr. Ben Carson's "Heart"-Warming Chili

Yield: 8 Servings

This chili is perfect for parties because it can be made ahead of time and tastes even better when reheated the next day. Serve the chili in ice cream sundae glasses. Put a layer of chili in the glasses first, then a layer of crushed baked corn chips, another layer of chili, a sprinkling of grated cheddar cheese and, finally, a swirl of sour cream and a cherry tomato. Pretty, nutritious and delicious! I guarantee there won't be any leftovers!

1 1/2 teaspoons virgin olive oil
  1   pound ground turkey
  1   medium-sized yellow onion, chopped
1/2   green bell pepper, diced
  1   stalk celery, chopped
  1   clove garlic, minced
  3   tablespoons canned tomato paste
1/2   teaspoon cornstarch
  1   tablespoon ground cumin
  1   tablespoon chili powder
1/2   teaspoon dried oregano
1/4   teaspoon freshly ground black pepper
  1   15-ounce can whole tomatoes, diced
  1   28-ounce can pinto beans

Heat the olive oil in a large Dutch oven or pot. Add the turkey, onion, bell pepper, celery, and garlic, and cook over low heat for 8 to 10 minutes, stirring occasionally. Raise the heat to medium and add the tomato paste and cornstarch, mixing well. Stir in the cumin, chili powder, oregano, black pepper, tomatoes, and beans. Reduce the heat to low and simmer the chili for 45 minutes, stirring occasionally.

Willie Mays' Home Run Bran Muffins

Yield: 12 muffins

"If you criticize a boy after a defeat, it sounds like blame. When you spell out his mistakes after the team has won, he learns." — Willie Mays, famous baseball player and businessman

   1 **tablespoon vegetable shortening, for greasing the pan**
   1 **cup oat bran**
   1 **cup whole-wheat flour**
   1 **cup skim milk**
   2 **eggs**
   3 **tablespoons honey**
   1 **tablespoon baking powder**
$1/2$ **teaspoon salt**
   1 **cup raisins**

Preheat the oven to 350 degrees. Grease 12 ($2^{1}/_{2}$-inch-deep) muffin cups with the shortening or use cup liners. Combine the oat bran, flour, milk, eggs, honey, baking powder, salt, and raisins in a large bowl and mix until well blended. Fill the muffin cups halfway to the top with the bran mixture and bake for 20 to 25 minutes, until the tops are golden brown and the muffins are cooked through.

Angela's By-the-Book Brittle

Yield: About 1 pound

Besides my other two cookbooks, I've written more than 50 children's books. I enjoy talking to my young audience and reading their work. I receive hundreds of letters every year from children who want to become authors "when they grow up." My advice, if you want to be a writer, write as often as you can! Practice makes perfect.

- 1 cup firmly packed brown sugar
- 1/4 cup light corn syrup
- 1/2 cup water
- 1 teaspoon salt
- 3/4 cup salted peanuts
- 2 tablespoons butter or margarine
- 1/4 teaspoon baking soda
- 5 cups crispy corn cereal squares, such as Chex

Grease a large cookie sheet. Combine the sugar, syrup, water, and salt in a heavy Dutch oven. Cook over medium heat, stirring constantly, until the mixture thickens (it should register about 250 degrees on a candy thermometer). Reduce the heat to low, add the peanuts, and mix well. Remove from heat. Add the butter and baking soda. Quickly stir in the cereal and then evenly spread the mixture out on the prepared cookie sheet. Cool. Break the brittle into pieces and store in an air-tight container in a cool place.

QUICK TIP: *Use sheets of white or brown butcher wrapping paper as a tablecloth. Pass out crayons and have your small guests color to their hearts' content.*

Carver's Peanut Butter Cookies

Yield: About 4 dozen cookies

"Since new developments are the products of a creative mind, we must therefore stimulate and encourage that type of mind in every way possible." — George Washington Carver, scientist, inventor, artist, educator

- 1 cup peanut butter
- 1 cup sugar
- 1 egg, beaten
- 1 teaspoon vanilla
- 3 tablespoons all-purpose flour

Preheat the oven to 350 degrees. Combine the peanut butter and sugar in a large bowl and mix well. Stir in the egg and vanilla. Roll the dough into small balls, about ³/₄ inches in diameter. Place the balls on an ungreased cookie sheet. Place the flour on a small plate. Dip a fork into the flour, then use the tines of the fork to flatten the balls. Bake for 10 minutes or until browned and cooked through. Allow the cookies to cool before removing them from the cookie sheet.

November

Thanksgiving Harvest Celebration Dinner

Thanksgiving has always been a special holiday for me. I cherish the time we spend before the meal giving thanks for all of our blessings. I'm especially thankful for my family. They are my biggest support system and a bottomless source of love. I enjoy gathering around the table with them as well as friends and eating a fabulous meal.

In Africa, it is traditional to have a "thanksgiving" celebration after the harvest. Yam festivals and other celebrations of thanksgiving have been held in parts of Africa for hundreds of years. The entire village participates, and sometimes the singing, dancing, and feasting lasts for a week. The festivals are not only a celebration of a bountiful harvest, but also of unity. It often takes the work of an entire village to bring in a good crop.

One of the most important West African crops is yams. They are not only an important food source but are also a lucky symbol for many people there. They are included in ceremonies from birth to death. The African yam is different from the American sweet potato which we mistakenly call yams here. African yams are thick, oblong tubers, often over a foot in length or longer. One giant African Igname yam often weighs as much as one hundred pounds. I think the African white yam tastes better than the American sweet potato, and is definitely a cause for celebration. Because of the lack of yams in this country, my ancestors substituted the sweet potato in their recipes. Today, when in season, African yams can often be found at grocery stores that carry ethnic foods.

The harvest maintained its importance to the captives even during the days of slavery. Shucking the corn crop became a time of celebration on many farms and plantations. Mrs. R. H. Marshall, a relative of President Millard Fillmore, wrote this account of a corn-shucking party in 1852:

> When the overseer has a quantity of corn to husk, he allows his Negroes to invite those on the neighboring plantations to come and help them in the evening. When all things are ready, they light the torches of pitch pine . . . and march while singing one of their corn songs to the spot. Then the captain mounts the heap of corn, and all sing a call song for the others to come, which is immediately answered from the other plantations, in a song that "they are coming." You can hear them distinctly for more than a mile. They sing as they march all the way, and when they arrive at the spot, they all join in one grand chorus . . . singing while those around them shuck and toss their corn into the crib . . . We waited until twelve o'clock and left them to enjoy their supper, prepared for them by their overseer.

I love maintaining traditions. I guess that's why I prepare basically the same Thanksgiving menu every year. With the world changing so rapidly, I enjoy clinging to the foods with which I grew up. I never realized until a few years ago that the sweet potatoes and corn that are traditional on most American Thanksgiving tables are also a part of my African-American ancestry.

THANKSGIVING HARVEST CELEBRATION DINNER MENU

DRINKS AND APPETIZERS

Almond Tea

Wilted Spinach Salad

MAIN DISHES

Roast Turkey with Peanut Sauce

Cornbread and Sage Dressing

Giblet Gravy

Baked Ham

SIDE DISHES

Stuffed Sweet Potatoes Southern Style

Green Beans with Almonds

Fried Corn

BREADS AND DESSERTS

Buttermilk Cornbread

Michael's Lemon Chess Pie

Almond Tea

Yield: 3 quarts

"If relatives help each other, what evil can hurt them?" — Ethiopian proverb

> 2 cups hot water
> 2 tablespoons lemon-flavored iced tea mix
> 1½ cups sugar
> 10 cups cold water
> 1 12-ounce can frozen lemonade concentrate, thawed
> 1 tablespoon almond extract
> 2 teaspoons vanilla

Pour the hot water into a medium container and stir in the tea mix. Set aside. Combine the sugar and 2 cups of the cold water in a large pot or Dutch oven, bring to a boil, and boil for 5 minutes. Stir in the tea mixture, the remaining 8 cups cold water, the lemonade, and the almond and vanilla extracts. Chill.

Wilted Spinach Salad

Yield: 4 to 6 Servings

You can make the dressing for the salad ahead of time, then reheat it and pour it over the salad just before serving.

2 pounds fresh spinach, stemmed, washed, dried, and cut into bite-sized pieces (see Note)
5 slices bacon
1 small yellow onion, chopped
$\frac{1}{2}$ cup red wine vinegar
1 to 2 teaspoons sugar
$\frac{1}{2}$ teaspoon Dijon mustard
Salt
Freshly ground black pepper

Divide the freshly washed spinach among individual salad plates. Set aside. Fry the bacon until crisp in a small skillet. Remove the bacon from the pan and set aside on paper towels to drain off some of the grease. Remove all but about 5 tablespoons of the bacon drippings from the pan. Add the onion to the drippings and sauté until tender and golden, 2 to 3 minutes. Stir in the red wine vinegar, sugar, and mustard. Stir until all of the ingredients are well blended and the sugar has dissolved. Add salt to taste.

Pour the hot dressing over the spinach. Garnish with crumbled bacon and freshly ground pepper.

NOTE: Spinach has a lovely, mild flavor but has a tendency to retain large amounts of sand and dirt. Improperly cleaned spinach will ruin a recipe.

When shopping for spinach, look for tender, bright green unblemished leaves. Remove and discard the roots and any leaves that are discolored. Let gravity work for you by allowing the spinach to sit in a basin full of cool water for several minutes. Most of the dirt will sink to the bottom of the basin. Remove the spinach and drain and rinse the basin. Repeat this washing process several times to remove all of the grit.

PREPARING A TURKEY FOR COOKING

To thaw out a frozen turkey ahead of time, remove it from the freezer 2 days before cooking and place it in a pan in the refrigerator. To thaw out a frozen turkey to use the same day, leave the turkey in its original wrapper, place it in a large container, and fill the container with cold water. (The water must be cold to prevent contamination.) Change the water every 30 minutes until the turkey is completely thawed out. Cook or refrigerate immediately; do not allow thawed turkey to stand at room temperature. Do not stuff the turkey the night before cooking as bacteria may grow inside the bird. Stuff the turkey immediately before cooking. Do not thaw commercially stuffed turkeys as bacteria will grow in the stuffing.

To clean the turkey, reach inside the chest cavity and remove the packet containing the neck, liver, and gizzards. Wash the turkey inside and out under cold running water. Pat dry and season for roasting.

Roast Turkey with Peanut Sauce

Yield: 10-12 Servings

African cooks use peanuts and peanut butter in dishes from soups to meat sauces. Rather than overpowering the taste of a dish (initially what I thought would happen), they enhance other flavors beautifully. This is also a great recipe for preparing turkey parts, or a turkey roast or roll; simply adjust the cooking time.

- ½ cup smooth peanut butter
- 2 tablespoons butter or margarine, softened
- 2 tablespoons poultry seasoning
- 1 tablespoon all-purpose flour
- ½ tablespoon salt
- 1 tablespoon sweet paprika
- 1 teaspoon freshly ground black pepper
- 1 teaspoon celery salt
- ⅓ cup lowfat milk
- 1 12- to 14-pound turkey, washed and patted dry
- 1 large yellow onion, chopped
- ½ cup chopped celery
- 2 14.5-ounce cans chicken broth

Preheat the oven to 325 degrees. Stir together the peanut butter, butter, poultry seasoning, flour, salt, paprika, black pepper and celery salt in a small bowl to make a paste. Stir in the milk, until the mixture is smooth.

Place the turkey in a large roasting pan. Rub the peanut paste all over the turkey, inside and out. Tuck the legs under the flap of skin around the tail and tuck the wing tips under the bird, tying with cord or string if necessary to hold in place. Place the chopped onion and celery inside the turkey.

Pour the chicken broth into the pan. Insert a meat thermometer into the thickest part of the thigh muscle, making sure the bulb does not touch the bone. Roast the turkey for $3^{1}/_{2}$ to $4^{1}/_{2}$ hours (18 to 20 minutes per pound), until the thermometer registers 185 to 190 degrees and the drumstick moves up and down easily. Baste the turkey and turn the pan every 30 minutes so that the turkey browns evenly on all sides. After about 3 hours, untuck or untie the wings and legs so they brown completely. Let the turkey stand at least 20 minutes before carving.

Cornbread and Sage Dressing

Yield: 8 Servings

The chopped cabbage in this recipe is my mother's secret ingredient. It releases water as it cooks and keeps everything moist. Serve the dressing as soon as possible after removing it from the oven and refrigerate leftovers immediately to prevent bacteria from forming.

3$^1/_2$ cups cornbread crumbs (see page 261 for cornbread recipe)
3$^1/_2$ cups soft bread crumbs
$^1/_2$ cup whole milk
4 tablespoons butter or margarine
$^1/_2$ cup finely chopped green cabbage
3 stalks celery, chopped
3 tablespoons minced yellow onion
2 cups turkey drippings or chicken broth
2 to 3 teaspoons ground sage
2 teaspoons salt
$^1/_2$ teaspoon ground savory seasoning
$^1/_2$ teaspoon freshly ground black pepper
1 egg, beaten

Preheat the oven to 400 degrees. Lightly grease a 2-quart ovenproof casserole dish. Place the bread crumbs in a large bowl. Add the milk and mix well.

Melt the butter in a saucepan over medium heat. Add the cabbage, celery, and onion, and sauté until tender but not brown, 3 to 5 minutes. Add the turkey drippings and heat for 5 minutes.

Add the onion mixture to the bread-crumb mixture, stirring well.

Add the sage, salt, savory seasoning, pepper, and egg to the bread-crumb mixture, stirring until all of the ingredients are well blended. Spoon the dressing into the prepared casserole dish, cover, and bake for 15 minutes or until the dressing is thoroughly heated. Serve warm.

Giblet Gravy

Yield: 2 ²/₃ cups

          Giblets and neck from 1 turkey
    1 small yellow onion, chopped
  4¼ cups water
    2 stalks celery, chopped
    2 hard-cooked eggs, chopped
    1 teaspoon salt
  ¼ teaspoon poultry seasoning
  ¼ teaspoon marjoram leaves
  ¼ teaspoon ground sage
  ¼ teaspoon ground thyme
  ¼ teaspoon freshly ground black pepper
    2 tablespoons cornstarch or flour

Combine the giblets, neck, onion, and 3 cups of the water in a medium saucepan and bring to a boil. Cover and reduce the heat to a low simmer for 45 minutes or until the giblets are fork-tender. Remove the giblets and neck from the broth, reserving the broth.

Remove the meat from the turkey neck. Chop the neck meat and giblets and return them to the broth. Add 1 cup of the water, the celery, eggs, salt, poultry seasoning, marjoram leaves, sage, thyme, and pepper to the broth and bring the mixture to a boil. Reduce the heat and simmer, uncovered, for 30 to 45 minutes.

Mix the cornstarch and the remaining ¼ cup of water in a small cup until smooth. Stir into the broth mixture. Bring the mixture to a boil, then boil and stir for 1 minute. Serve the hot gravy with the turkey and dressing.

Baked Ham

Yield: 16 to 18 Servings

The brown sugar, mustard, and sherry mixture add a sweet flavor and a beautiful glaze to the ham. I prepare this recipe throughout the year for company. For an elegant look, I decorate the glazed ham with pineapple slices and marashino cherries.

10-12 lb whole, uncooked, smoked ham
1 16-ounce package light-brown sugar
1 tablespoon brown mustard
1/4 cup sherry or orange-juice
Whole cloves

Preheat the oven to 325 degrees. Rinse off the ham and wipe it dry with paper towels. Place ham in pan, fat side up, in a foil-lined shallow baking pan. Bake, uncovered, for 2 hours. Stir together the brown sugar, sherry, and mustard in a medium bowl to make a smooth paste.

Remove the ham from the oven and pour off the drippings. Use a knife to remove any skin from the ham. Score the ham in a diamond pattern by making 1/4 inch diagonal cuts 1 1/4 inches apart in the fat; do not cut into the meat. Spread the brown sugar mixture over the surface of the ham. Place a clove in the center of each diamond shape. Return the ham to the oven to continue baking for another 30 minutes or until a meat thermometer registers 140 degrees. Remove the ham from the oven and allow it to stand at least 20 minutes before slicing.

Stuffed Sweet Potatoes Southern Style

Yield: 8 Servings

This unusual recipe can be prepared up to the point when the Swiss cheese is sprinkled on the stuffed potatoes. The potatoes can then be refrigerated or frozen until you are ready to defrost and bake them.

1 10-ounce package frozen collard greens or 1 cup cooked collards
4 medium-sized sweet potatoes
6 slices bacon
4 green onions sliced, including tops
$1/2$ cup heavy cream
$1/2$ cup freshly grated Parmesan cheese
4 tablespoons butter or margarine, softened
$1/2$ teaspoon cayenne pepper
$1/2$ teaspoon salt
1 cup finely grated Swiss cheese

Preheat the oven to 350 degrees. Cook the frozen collard greens according to the package directions. Drain well.

Arrange the sweet potatoes on a baking sheet or in a baking pan and bake until fork-tender, 1 to $1^1/2$ hours. When the sweet potatoes are cool enough to handle, slice each one lengthwise, carefully hollow out the inside with a spoon, and place the flesh in a large bowl. Set the potato shells aside.

Fry the bacon until crisp in a large skillet, then transfer to a paper towel to drain, reserving the drippings in the skillet. Add the green onions and collard greens to the bacon fat and sauté over medium heat for 2 minutes. Add the greens mixture to the sweet potato flesh in the bowl. Crumble the bacon and add it to the bowl along with the cream, Parmesan, butter, cayenne pepper, and salt. Using an electric mixer or hand masher, whip the potato mixture until smooth. Place spoonfuls of the potato mixture into the sweet potato shells, mounding it in the center. Top the stuffed sweet potatoes with the Swiss cheese. Bake for 20 to 30 minutes, until the potatoes are heated and the cheese has melted.

Green Beans with Almonds

Yield: 8 Servings

"Black people, both during and after the slave era, have been compelled to build, creatively and often improvisationally, a family life consistent with the dictates of survival." — Angela Y. Davis, activist

    3 10-ounce packages frozen cut green beans
    4 tablespoons butter or margarine
    1 cup sliced almonds, toasted (see Note on page 93)
1½ teaspoons salt
 ½ teaspoon ground oregano

Cook the green beans according to the package directions. Drain. Melt the butter in a medium skillet. Add the almonds, stirring to coat them with the butter. Add the green beans, salt, and oregano, mixing well. Cook for 2 minutes to warm.

Fried Corn

Yield: 8 Servings

Fried corn has become my sister Sandra's specialty. Some recipes call for bacon fat instead of butter, but she and I think butter gives the corn a better flavor.

> $3/4$ cup butter
> 4 cups fresh or frozen corn kernels, thawed
> 1 cup sugar
> $1/2$ teaspoon salt

Melt $1/2$ cup of the butter in a medium skillet. Add the corn, sugar, and salt and stir well. Dot with the remaining $1/4$ cup butter. Simmer over low heat for 15 minutes, stirring frequently.

Buttermilk Cornbread

Yield: 2 pans

The secret to good dressing is good cornbread. This recipe yields two pans of cornbread, one to use in the dressing and one to serve. Each pan of bread will serve about 9 people.

3 cups cornmeal
1 cup all-purpose flour
4 teaspoons baking powder
2 teaspoons sugar
2 teaspoons salt
1 teaspoon baking soda
$\frac{1}{2}$ cup vegetable shortening or bacon fat
3 cups buttermilk
4 eggs

Preheat the oven to 450 degrees. Grease two 8-inch square or 9-inch round baking pans. Combine the cornmeal, flour, baking powder, sugar, salt, baking soda, shortening, buttermilk, and eggs in a large bowl. Beat with an electric mixer on high speed for 30 seconds. Pour the batter into the prepared baking pans and bake until golden brown, 25 to 30 minutes.

Michael's Lemon Chess Pie

Yield: 8 Servings

This is my husband Michael's favorite dessert. I usually prepare it for his birthday, for Thanksgiving and, of course, upon demand. I love this pie too, especially as a light, refreshing finish for a heavy meal.

>   4 eggs, at room temperature
> 1/2 cup butter, softened
> 1 1/2 cups sugar
>   1 tablespoon all-purpose flour
>   Pinch of salt
>   2 tablespoons freshly squeezed lemon juice
>   1 teaspoon vanilla
>   1 9-inch Party Pastry, unbaked (page 111)

Preheat the oven to 325 degrees. Cream together the eggs and butter in a medium bowl until fluffy. Add the sugar, flour, and salt, mixing well. Stir in the lemon juice and vanilla. Pour the filling into the pie shell and bake until filling sets and the center is firm, about 35 minutes.

December

An Old-Fashioned Christmas Dinner

Christmas is like a present for the senses. I love the sight of twinkling lights, Christmas trees, and children's faces in a Christmas play. I love to hear the scriptures about the birth of the Christ child, Christmas carols, and the crackle of logs on a fire. I love the smell of cedar and cinnamon, and the feeling of velvet dresses and woolen gloves.

In times of slavery, African-Americans looked forward to Christmas because the field workers were often given a week's rest from their labors, and many slaves took the opportunity to escape to freedom. In the big house, the slaves probably worked even harder than usual, fixing the Christmas feast and preparing the house for guests.

In many parts of the South during slavery times, people played a game called Christmas Gift. Whenever two people met on Christmas morning, the usual good morning greeting was replaced with rapid greetings of "Christmas Gift." Whoever said the greeting first was given a small present, usually cookies, candies, or other treats. You may want to play this old-fashioned game on Christmas morning with your family.

Sometimes the slave master brought the slaves together to distribute gifts, usually clothes. Eggnog was often passed out to the adults, along with permission to take meat from the smokehouse for Christmas dinner. Then the slaves gathered in their quarters for a short religious service and the singing of hymns, after which they began cooking their Christmas feast. Hams, chickens, squirrels, possums, sweet potatoes, cabbage, wild greens, corncakes, and homemade persimmon wine were usually on the menu. The Christmas feast was a welcome change from the cornmeal and rancid meats the slaves were ordinarily given to eat. In order to survive, they supplemented with vegetables grown on small patches of land near their quarters, wild greens, and fish and game. After dinner, the adults gave homemade gifts, such as aprons, baskets, or quilts to the children.

Along the North Carolina coast and in some other parts of the South, after dinner everyone went to see the John Konny performers, male slaves dressed in wild costumes who danced, sang, and paraded long into the night. The John Konny tradition appears to have originated in West Africa and is thought to take its name from John Connu or Conny, who was the head of a tribe located on the Guinea Coast around 1720.

The entertainers were allowed to roam from one farm and plantation to another, dressed in elaborate costumes made of rags, feathers, net, animals horns, fur, and strange masks. "John Konny" was the leader of the parade and usually wore a headdress that made him seven feet tall. A loud, bone-jarring rhythm was beat out on a "deal box" or "gumba box," a wooden-framed instrument covered by tanned animal hide. Cow horns were blown; the jaw bones of animals were rattled; and bells, whistles, and crude triangles were played as the revelers paraded from one place to another.

Variations of the name John Konny appear in historical texts.

John Konny is the Jamaican name, but the gala has been referred to as Johnkankus, John Connu, and John Koner or Kuner in America. Gombe dancers in Bermuda perform at their John Konny festivals, and the elaborate tradition of using costumes, instruments, and fire-dancing continues at Jamaican Christmas celebrations.

The John Konny tradition died out for the most part among African-Americans around 1863, but was embraced by white Southerners until the early 1900s.

Whether Christmas is celebrated with old-fashioned customs, family traditions, or a modern twist, it is a wonderful time for gathering the family together. I love cooking delicious dishes for my family and preparing homemade gifts from my kitchen for my friends. This menu is sure to put your family and guests in a merry mood, from the first glass of eggnog to the last piece of fruitcake.

AN OLD-FASHIONED CHRISTMAS DINNER MENU

DRINKS AND APPETIZERS

Southern Wassail Punch

Christmas Salad

MAIN DISH

Pork Loin Roast with Savory Gravy

SIDE DISHES

Sesame Asparagus

Creamy Garlic Mashed Potatoes

Baked Onions Stuffed with Oyster Dressing

BREADS AND DESSERTS

Spoon Rolls

Old-Fashioned Fruitcake

Hot Fudge Cake with Vanilla Ice Cream

Quick-and-Easy Fudge

Southern Wassail Punch

Yield: 12 Servings

"And in the sixth month the angel Gabriel was sent from God unto a city of Galilee, named Nazareth. To a virgin espoused to a man whose name was Joseph, of the house of David; and the virgin's name was Mary." — St. Luke 1:26–27

- ½ gallon apple cider or apple juice
- ½ cup firmly packed brown sugar
- 1 3-ounce can frozen lemonade, thawed and undiluted
- 1 3-ounce can frozen orange juice, thawed and undiluted
- ½ tablespoon whole cloves
- ½ tablespoon whole allspice
- 12 1-inch cinnamon sticks

Mix the cider, sugar, lemonade, and orange juice together in a large pot. Place the cloves and allspice in a cheesecloth bag, tie the open end tightly, and add it to the cider mixture. Cover the pot and simmer for 15 minutes. Remove and discard the spice bag. Ladle the hot punch into cups garnished with a cinnamon stick.

Christmas Salad

Yield: 8 Servings

"And Joseph also went up from Galilee, out of the city of Nazareth, into Judaea, unto the city of David, which is called Bethlehem; (because he was of the house and lineage of David:) To be taxed with Mary his espoused wife, being great with child." — St. Luke 2:4–5

 2 pounds bean sprouts
 1 pound button mushrooms, sliced
 2 cups artichokes hearts, drained and chopped
 2 cups sliced cucumbers
 2 tomatoes, sliced
 6 green onions with tops, sliced
 1/4 cup salad oil
 1/4 cup white wine vinegar
 2 small cloves garlic, crushed
 1 teaspoon dry mustard
 1/2 teaspoon oregano
 1/2 teaspoon salt
 1/2 teaspoon freshly ground black pepper
 4 cups mixed salad greens (shredded cabbage, endive, watercress, spinach, romaine, or other lettuce)

Combine the bean sprouts, mushrooms, artichoke hearts, cucumbers, tomatoes, and green onions in a medium bowl. Place the oil, vinegar, garlic, dry mustard, oregano, salt, and pepper in the bowl of a food processor or blender and blend until smooth. Pour the dressing over the prepared vegetables, tossing well to coat. Cover and chill for at least an hour. Serve over the salad greens.

Pork Loin Roast with Savory Gravy

Yield: 8 Servings

"And she brought forth her firstborn son, and wrapped him in swaddling clothes, and laid him in a manger; because there was no room for them in the inn." — St. Luke 2:7

1	4- to 5-pound pork loin roast
1	teaspoon salt
1/2	teaspoon freshly ground black pepper
1/2	teaspoon dried thyme leaves
1	bay leaf, crushed
4	tablespoons all-purpose flour
2	medium-sized yellow onions, chopped
1	carrot, cut into 1/2-inch slices
1	stalk celery, chopped
7 to 8	large sprigs fresh parsley
3 to 4	cups water
1/3	cup firmly packed brown sugar
2	tablespoons all-purpose flour

Preheat the oven to 350 degrees. Rub the roast with salt, pepper, thyme, and bay leaf. Dust the roast with 2 tablespoons of the flour. Place the meat in a roasting pan, fat side up. Surround the roast with the onions, carrot, celery, and parsley. Pour 2 cups of water into the pan. Cook the roast for 2½ hours, basting every 30 minutes and adding extra water to the pan as needed. During the last 30 minutes of the cooking time, sprinkle the roast with the brown sugar.

To make the gravy, remove the roast and vegetables from the

roasting pan and strain the pan drippings into a saucepan. Combine the remaining 2 tablespoons flour with 1½ cups of water in a small bowl and mix until smooth. Add the flour mixture to the pan drippings and cook over medium heat, stirring constantly, until the gravy has thickened, 5 to 8 minutes. Serve the gravy with the roast and vegetables.

Sesame Asparagus

Yield: 6 Servings

"And, lo, the star, which they saw in the east, went before them, till it came and stood over where the young child was." — St. Matthew 2:9

1 cup water
1 teaspoon salt
2 pounds fresh asparagus, washed and cut diagonally
   into 1¹/₂-inch lengths
3 tablespoons virgin olive oil
¹/₄ cup minced yellow onion
3 tablespoons toasted sesame seeds (page 93)
1 teaspoon freshly ground black pepper

Fill a medium saucepan with the water and ¹/₂ teaspoon of the salt and bring to a boil. Add all of the asparagus except for the tips to the boiling water and cook for 6 minutes. Add the tips, cover, and cook for another 5 to 8 minutes or until the tips are crisp-tender. Drain and set the asparagus aside.

Heat the oil in a large skillet. Add the asparagus and onion and sauté for 2 to 3 minutes. Sprinkle with the sesame seeds, pepper, and the remaining ¹/₂ teaspoon salt. Mix well and serve hot.

Creamy Garlic Mashed Potatoes

Yield: 6 Servings

4 or 5 large baking potatoes
1½ teaspoons salt, to taste
1 cup milk
3 tablespoons butter or margarine
1½ teaspoons freshly ground white pepper
1 head of garlic, peeled, braised, and puréed (see Note)

Wash, peel, and quarter the potatoes and place them in a pot with one teaspoon of the salt, and cover them with water. Bring to a boil and loosely place a cover on top of the pot. Continue to boil until the potatoes are done and slightly firm but easily pierced with a fork. Drain and discard the water in the pot. Shake the pot back and forth over low heat to remove any remaining moisture, 10 to 15 seconds (a film will build up in the pan when the moisture has evaporated).

Warm ½ cup of the milk in a small pan over medium heat for 30 seconds; set aside. While still warm, place the potatoes in a large mixing bowl. Whip the potatoes, the remaining salt, ¼ cup of the warm milk, 2 tablespoons of the butter, and the pepper together until mixture begins to become creamy, about 3 to 5 minutes. Add the puréed garlic, the remaining ¼ cup of the warm milk and the tablespoon of butter and continue to whip the potatoes until smooth and free of lumps.

NOTE: To peel the head of garlic, drop it into a pot of boiling water for 30 seconds, drain, then run cold water over it. Rub the cloves gently with your fingers until the skin slips off. Place the peeled garlic in a pan with $1/2$ cup of the milk and simmer over low heat for 5 to 10 minutes until the garlic becomes tender and creamy. Purée the garlic in the bowl of a food processor for 10 to 20 seconds.

Baked Onions Stuffed with Oyster Dressing

Yield: 6 Servings

The onions add extra flavor to the oyster dressing and when baked, they look beautiful placed around the pork roast.

- 6 large yellow onions, washed and peeled
- 1/2 teaspoon salt
- 1 cup chopped oysters, undrained
- 1 cup Ritz cracker crumbs
- 1/4 cup finely chopped green bell pepper
- 3 tablespoons butter, melted
- 3/4 teaspoon poultry seasoning
- 1 cup water

Preheat the oven to 350 degrees. Place the onions and salt in a large pot of water, boiling for 20 minutes or until firm but slightly tender when pierced with a fork. Drain the onions, cool, and carefully hollow them out out with a paring knife. Set the hollowed-out onion shells aside. Chop the core of the onion finely and set aside.

To make the oyster dressing, combine the oysters, 2/3 cup of the cracker crumbs, the bell pepper, 2 tablespoons of the melted butter, the poultry seasoning, and the chopped onion in a small bowl. Stuff the onion shells with the dressing, mounding the remaining dressing on top. Mix the remaining cracker crumbs with the tablespoon of butter in a small bowl. Place the crumbs on top of the stuffed onions. Place the water in the bottom of a shallow baking pan. Place the onions in the water and bake for 45 minutes or until the onions are tender and the tops are a golden brown.

Spoon Rolls

Yield: 2 dozen rolls

The dough for these easy-to-make rolls is spooned into muffin cups, thus their name. The dough can be prepared ahead of time and stored in an airtight container in the refrigerator for several days.

    1 **package active dry yeast**
    2 **cups warm water (105 to 115 degrees)**
  3/4 **cup butter or margarine, melted**
  1/4 **cup sugar**
    1 **egg**
    4 **cups self-rising flour**

Preheat the oven to 350 degrees. Lightly grease the bottoms of the cups in two 12-cup muffin tins. Dissolve the yeast in the water in a small bowl. Set aside.

Combine the butter, sugar, and egg in a large bowl and beat until well blended. Stir in the yeast mixture. Continue mixing while stirring in the flour, a small amount at a time, until the mixture is smooth and a soft dough forms. Spoon the dough into the prepared muffin tins, filling the cups two-thirds of the way to the top. Bake for 25 minutes or until lightly browned.

FLOUR

Old-Fashioned Fruitcake

Yield: 10-inch cake

Make this cake several weeks ahead of time and store it in the refrigerator so that the flavors have time to mingle.

       1 cup butter or margarine, softened
   2$^{1}/_{4}$ cups sugar
       6 eggs
       3 tablespoons brandy extract
       4 cups all-purpose flour
    $^{1}/_{2}$ teaspoon baking powder
   1$^{1}/_{2}$ teaspoons salt
   1$^{1}/_{2}$ teaspoons ground cinnamon
       1 teaspoon ground nutmeg
       6 cups (about 1$^{1}/_{2}$ pounds) chopped pecans
   4$^{1}/_{2}$ cups (about 1$^{1}/_{2}$ pounds) mixed candied fruit and peel, chopped
       1 15-ounce box golden raisins
          Honey

Preheat the oven to 275 degrees. Lightly grease a 10-inch tube pan. Cream the butter and sugar in a large bowl until light and fluffy. Add the eggs, one at a time, beating well after each addition. Stir in the brandy flavoring.

Sift together the flour, baking powder, and salt in a large bowl. Stir in the cinnamon, nutmeg, pecans, 4 cups of the fruit and peel, and the raisins. Add the fruit mixture to the creamed ingredients and mix well. Spoon the batter into the prepared pan and bake for 2$^{1}/_{2}$ to 3 hours or until a toothpick or cake tester inserted into the center of the cake comes out clean. Thirty minutes before the cake is done, remove it from the oven, brush the top with honey, and sprinkle it with the remaining 1/2 cup fruit and peel.

Cool the cake on a wire rack, then remove it from the pan. Wrap the cake tightly in aluminum foil and refrigerate for several weeks before serving.

Hot Fudge Cake with Vanilla Ice Cream

Yield: 9-inch Cake

"And shalt call his name JESUS. He shall be great, and shall be called the Son of the Highest: and the Lord God shall give unto him the throne of his father David: And he shall reign over the house of Jacob for ever; and of his kingdom there shall be no end."
— St. Luke 1:31–33

> 1 cup all-purpose flour
> 2 teaspoons baking powder
> 1/4 teaspoon salt
> 3/4 cup sugar
> 1/4 cup plus 2 1/2 tablespoons cocoa
> 1/2 cup milk
> 2 tablespoons vegetable shortening, melted
> 1 teaspoon vanilla
> 1 cup chopped walnuts
> 3/4 cup firmly packed brown sugar
> 1 3/4 cups hot water
> 1 quart vanilla ice cream

Preheat the oven to 350 degrees. Lightly grease a 9-inch square pan. Sift the flour, baking powder, and salt into a large bowl. Add the sugar, 2 1/2 tablespoons of the cocoa, the milk, shortening, and vanilla, and stir until the batter is smooth. Stir in the walnuts. Spread the batter into the prepared pan and sprinkle with the brown sugar and the remaining 1/4 cup cocoa. Pour the water over the mixture. DO NOT STIR. Bake for 45 minutes. The texture of this cake is a cross between a pudding and a cake so a tester will not come out clean. Cut the cake into squares. Serve with a scoop of ice cream and with the sauce left in the pan.

Quick-And-Easy Fudge

Yield: 2 to 3 dozen candies

Place this fudge in a pretty gift box, a basket decorated with a bow, or a festive metal container and give it away when playing the Christmas Gift game or another holiday celebration. It makes a sweet present.

> **Butter or margarine, for greasing the pan**
> 1   **14-ounce can sweetened condensed milk**
> 1   **12-ounce package semisweet chocolate chips**
> 1   **teaspoon vanilla**
> 1½ **cups chopped walnuts**

Grease an 8-inch-square pan. Combine the milk and the chocolate chips in a medium saucepan over low heat and stir until the chocolate is melted and the mixture is smooth. Remove from the heat and stir in the vanilla and nuts. Spread the mixture evenly in the prepared pan and refrigerate for 1 hour or until firm. Cut into small squares.

Kwanzaa Karamu Feast

At our house, we celebrate Thanksgiving, Christmas, and Kwanzaa, an African-American cultural holiday. Kwanzaa was created in 1966 by Dr. Maulana "Ron" Karenga as a way of unifying the African-American family and community through a celebration based on our African heritage. Food is a big part of most celebrations, and Kwanzaa is no different. Kwanzaa is sort of like an African-American thanksgiving celebration. During the seven day holiday, I cook recipes that contain ingredients used by African cooks as a way of honoring our ancestral heritage.

Focusing on ways we can improve ourselves, help others, and secure our future as a family and as a community is a large part of the Kwanzaa celebration. We study a different Kwanzaa principle, called the Nguzo Saba, in the African language of Swahili, each day of the celebration, which begins on December 26 and ends on January 1. The seven principles are unity, self-determination, collective work and responsibility, cooperative economics, purpose, creativity, and faith. We make a pledge each day to "pull together" to achieve our goals.

Kwanzaa is a wonderful time to explore and share our culture with our family and friends. The principles upon which Kwanzaa is based can help to sustain us throughout the year. I especially enjoy the Karamu feast which is held on the sixth day of Kwanzaa, December 31. The Karamu is a feast which gathers together family and friends to celebrate our culture, our ancestors, and the community. A program is presented, gifts are exchanged, and a wonderful variety of foods are served, usually rooted in African culture.

If you haven't participated in Kwanzaa festivities in the past, you may want to celebrate the holiday this year, or you may want to join in the Kwanzaa activities in your community. If there is a community-wide Karamu feast, you may want to bring one of the dishes on the suggested menu. The recipes can stand alone if you're only required to bring one item or work well together if you're hosting the Karamu feast.

KWANZAA KARAMU FEAST MENU

DRINKS AND APPETIZERS

Karamu Warmer

Soul Food Dip

MAIN DISH

West African Couscous

VEGETABLES

Baked Cheddar Tomatoes

Okra Fingers

BREADS AND DESSERTS

Bacon-Cheese Bread

Lemon Pecan Cake

Karamu Warmer

Yield: 2¹/₂ quarts

UMOJA (UNITY): *To strive for and maintain unity in the family, community, nation, and race.*

> 2 quarts apple juice
> 2 cups canned orange juice
> 1¹/₂ cups pineapple juice
> 1 cup lemon juice
> ¹/₂ cup sugar
> 1 stick cinnamon
> 1 teaspoon whole cloves

Combine the apple, orange, pineapple, and lemon juices, sugar, cinnamon, and cloves in a large Dutch oven or pot and simmer over low heat for 30 minutes. Strain and serve hot.

Soul Food Dip

Yield: 3 cups

KUJICHAGULIA (SELF-DETERMINATION): *To define ourselves, name ourselves, create for ourselves, and speak for ourselves instead of being defined, named, created for, and spoken for by others.*

- 2 tablespoons butter or margarine
- 1/2 medium onion, diced
- 1/2 cup diced celery
- 1 10-ounce package frozen, chopped turnip greens
- 1 teaspoon salt
- 1 teaspoon freshly ground black pepper
- 1/4 teaspoon freshly grated lemon zest
- 1 10³/₄-ounce can cream of mushroom soup
- 1 3-ounce can sliced mushrooms, drained
- 1 6-ounce package cream cheese spread
- 1/2 teaspoon garlic powder
- 1 teaspoon Worcestershire sauce
- 5 drops hot sauce

Melt the butter in a large saucepan. Add the onion and celery and sauté until the onion is golden brown and the celery is tender. Set aside.

Cook the turnip greens in a small pot according to the package directions. Drain well and season with salt and pepper. Using a blender or food processor, grind the turnip greens and lemon zest together until smooth.

Add the turnip greens, soup, mushrooms, cheese spread, garlic powder, Worcestershire sauce, and hot sauce to the sautéed vegetables and cook over medium heat, stirring constantly, until the cheese melts and the ingredients are blended.

West African Couscous

Yield: 6 to 8 Servings

UJIMA (COLLECTIVE WORK AND RESPONSIBILITY): *To build and maintain our community together and make our sisters' and brothers' problems our problems and to solve them together.*

- $1/2$ cup peanut or salad oil
- 2 medium-sized yellow onions, sliced
- 1 4- to 5-pound roasting chicken, cut into 8 pieces, washed and patted dry
- 2 teaspoons turmeric
- 1 teaspoon ground cumin
- 1 teaspoon ground allspice
- 1 teaspoon salt
- $1^{1}/_{2}$ teaspoons cayenne pepper
- 2 cloves garlic, crushed
- 3 bay leaves
- 2 $10^{1}/_{2}$-ounce cans condensed chicken broth
- 3 carrots, peeled and halved crosswise
- 3 white turnips, peeled and cut into quarters
- 1 small head cabbage, cut into wedges
- 1 small eggplant, sliced crosswise into $1/2$-inch pieces
- 3 zucchini, sliced
- 1 16-ounce can chickpeas, drained
- 2 cups hot water
- 1 cup dark raisins
- 1 16-ounce package couscous or semolina
- $1/2$ cup butter or margarine, melted

Heat the oil over medium heat in a large Dutch oven. Add the onion and sauté until tender, about 3 minutes, then remove from the pot. Add the chicken to the oil and cook for 15 to 20 minutes, turning on all sides to brown evenly. Add the onions, 1 ½ teaspoons of the turmeric, the cumin, allspice, salt, cayenne pepper, garlic, bay leaves, and chicken broth. Mix well. Add the carrots, turnips, and cabbage. Cover and cook for 20 minutes. Add the eggplant and zucchini and cook for another 20 minutes. Add the chickpeas, cover, and cook for another 5 minutes.

Meanwhile, in a small bowl, pour the hot water over the raisins. Set aside until raisins are moist and plump. Prepare the couscous according to the instructions on the package. Drain the raisins and add them to the couscous. Mix in the butter and the remaining ½ teaspoon turmeric. Mound the couscous in the center of a large serving platter. Arrange the chicken and vegetables around the couscous. Transfer the remaining sauce to a gravy boat and serve on the side.

Baked Cheddar Tomatoes

Yield: 10 Servings

UJAMAA: CO-OPERATIVE ECONOMICS: *To build and maintain our own stores, shops, and other businesses and profit from them together.*

    5 medium tomatoes
       Virgin olive oil
    3/4 teaspoon salt
    1 cup soft bread crumbs
    1 cup (4 ounces) shredded Cheddar cheese
    4 tablespoons butter or margarine, melted
    1 teaspoon dried whole basil
    1/2 teaspoon cayenne pepper

Preheat the oven to 350 degrees. Cut the tomatoes in half crosswise. Brush with the olive oil and sprinkle with the salt. Place the tomatoes, cut side up, in a 13 × 9-inch baking dish. Combine the bread crumbs, cheddar cheese, butter, basil, and cayenne pepper in a medium bowl. Spoon the bread crumb mixture on top of the tomatoes. Bake for 12 to 15 minutes or until the tomatoes are hot and the cheese melts.

Okra Fingers

Yield: 8 Servings

NIA (PURPOSE): *To make our collective vocation the building and developing of our community in order to restore our people to their traditional greatness.*

40 small fresh okra pods, washed, stems trimmed, and patted dry
2 cups buttermilk
1¼ cups all-purpose flour
½ cup cornmeal
2 teaspoons baking powder
1 teaspoon salt
¼ teaspoon cayenne pepper
Vegetable oil, for frying

Place the okra in a shallow container. Pour the buttermilk over the okra. Set aside. Combine the flour, cornmeal, baking powder, salt and pepper on a plate, mixing well. Roll the okra pods in the flour mixture until coated on all sides.

Heat the oil for frying to 375 degrees in a deep skillet. Place the okra in the hot oil and fry for 3 minutes. Turn the okra once and fry for another 2 to 3 minutes or until lightly brown. Drain on paper towels.

Bacon-Cheese Bread

Yield: 8 to 10 slices

KUUMBA (CREATIVITY): *To do always as much as we can, in the way we can, in order to leave our community more beautiful and beneficial than we inherited it.*

     1 large loaf unsliced French bread
     6 tablespoons butter or margarine, softened
     4 green onions, finely chopped
     3 tablespoons mustard
     2 teaspoons poppy seeds
     4 ounces Swiss cheese, cut into 6 slices
2 or 3 slices bacon

Preheat the oven to 350 degrees. Slice the bread diagonally and trim off the crust. Combine 4 tablespoons of the butter, the green onions, mustard, and poppy seeds in a small bowl. Spread the butter mixture on both sides of the bread slices. Place a slice of cheese on top of each slice, trimming the cheese so that it does not extend over the edge of the bread. Press the bread slices together into a loaf. Spread the top of the loaf with the remaining butter or margarine. Lay the bacon slices on top of the bread. Wrap the loaf in aluminum foil and bake for 30 to 40 minutes or until the bread is slightly brown on the edges.

Lemon Pecan Cake

Yield: 10-inch cake

IMANI (FAITH): *To believe with all our heart in our people, our parents, our teachers, our leaders, and the righteousness and victory of our struggle.*

       1 **cup chopped pecans**
      3/4 **cup butter or margarine, softened**
    1 1/2 **cups sugar**
       3 **eggs, beaten**
       3 **cups all-purpose flour**
       3 **teaspoons baking powder**
      1/2 **teaspoon salt**
       1 **cup milk**
          Juice and zest of 1 lemon

Preheat the oven to 375 degrees. Grease a 10-inch tube pan and sprinkle the bottom with the chopped nuts. Cream the butter and sugar in a large bowl until fluffy. Add the eggs and mix well.

Sift the flour, baking powder, and salt into a large bowl. Alternately and a small amount at a time, add the milk and the flour mixture to the egg mixture. Mix until well blended. Stir in lemon juice and zest. Pour the batter in the prepared pan and bake for 1 hour or until a cake tester or toothpick inserted into the cake comes out clean. Cool on a wire rack, then remove from the pan.

Index